BRAINIAC

FORTHCOMING TITLES

De La Soul by Dave Heaton

AFI by Andi Coulter

BRAINIAC

Justin Vellucci

J-Card Press

COPYRIGHT © 2024 BY JUSTIN VELLUCCI

All rights reserved. This book or any portion thereof may not be reproduced or used in any manner whatsoever without the express written permission of the publisher except for the use of brief quotations in a book review.

ISBN: 979-8-9891947-0-4 (print)
ISBN: 979-8-9891947-1-1 (ebook)

Library of Congress Control Number: 2024934859

J-Card Press
460 Center Street #6578
Moraga, California 94570

Cover photo: Martyn Goodacre/Getty Images
Interior design: Milton Fine
Author photo: Inbal K. Vellucci

www.jcardpress.com

CONTENTS

Prologue: "A disaster scenario I cannot have" 1
1. "Like Devo on acid" 7
Musical interlude: "Superdupersonic" 19
2. A history of buckeyes 23
Musical interlude: "I, Fuzzbot" 31
3. "Just kind of took off from there" 35
Musical interlude: "Sexual Frustration" 61
4. "Ride yourself away, each and every day" 65
Musical interlude: "Hot Metal Doberman's" 87
5. "They were just getting bigger and bigger" 89
Musical interlude: "Go Freaks Go" 101
6. "Everybody believed in what we were doing" 103
Musical interlude: "Vincent Come on Down" 111
7. "Don't melt me down till the crisis is over" 115
Musical interlude: "70 kg Man" 123
8. "Electronic. And so aggressive." 125
Musical interlude: "Fresh New Eyes" 137
9. "I want this to mean something" 139
Epilogue: "Something's gotta give" 161
Chapter notes 171

PROLOGUE: "A DISASTER SCENARIO I CANNOT HAVE"

You sit down hungry to remember and slide your fingers along the rictus of the sleeve's mouth, pulling out that familiar twelve-inch black vinyl disc. Then, gently, you place the EP on the circular platter and lower the thin mechanical arm.

As the needle begins to trace well-worn grooves in wax, the vinyl ever revolving, you start to remember the story.

The soundtrack of your life, once again, is curated by Brainiac.

On the record's too-short closing track, the synthesized drums glitch and shuffle, less a percussive heartbeat than the death rattle of some demented machine. After a few measures, the band enters the frame in a slightly off-kilter B minor, setting up the musical scaffolding. Drummer Tyler Trent snaps out a simple 4/4 march on his snare.

Then we meet front man Tim Taylor.

"I know how it feels when I need a disaster scenario I cannot have," Taylor croons, his voice sensual but also vaguely menacing, his presence already breeding an unusual magnetism.

BRAINIAC

"My magic hand smacks me in the forehead and reminds me I can be so bad."

It was the spring of 1997, moments before Memorial Day weekend.

Brainiac had wrapped up a practice session in the band's rehearsal space under the 1470 West club in Kettering, a suburb five miles south of Dayton, Ohio. Taylor—the quartet's lead singer, primary songwriter and, before the age of thirty, already a road-tested musical polymath—stayed late into the evening to flesh out a few new songs.

The group had been developing, among other pieces, three highly melodic and guitar-driven tracks for its much-anticipated fourth LP. At least two major labels were lying in wait for the band's next move.

Taylor left 1470 West at about 3:00 a.m.

Before Taylor's insinuation of danger even takes hold, bassist Juan Monasterio interrupts the conversation with a poppy fill—just five simple notes. And then Brainiac erupts, all four members now fully engaged in a punctuating groove.

"Would you believe me if I said it was easy to file away my better half?" Taylor continues. "Lock me in a closet with my mittens on and watch me while I blow my stack—oh! Wha-oh!"

Expectations were running high for Brainiac.

The group recently had returned from opening for Beck on a six-date tour in Europe. Nine days earlier, they had played a set in England with the California-bred musician, the man behind *Odelay* sizing up superstardom like the fit of a well-tailored suit.

The chatter from major labels courting Brainiac was growing to a fever pitch. Elektra and Interscope led the roaring. Rumor had it that Rick Rubin had been penciled in to produce their next record. Others were name-dropping Nine Inch Nails' Trent Reznor. A tour had been booked with Rage Against the Machine.

You don't even see the punch coming.

Taylor's delivery is scene-setting; it drives forward the entire song. But he's also seducing you, getting you comfortable, giving you another drink so you can decompress a bit.

He wants you to let down your guard.

"When I have no pain, I stand on my hands and wait for the pain to come," he sings in the second verse's closing couplet. "I guess I'll have to give my finger puppets up / Tell me if you want one."

Pause, 2, 3, 4—then the chorus erupts and the band lunges forward as one tangled mess of sound.

"Mr. Fingers, I argue and look like a fool / Get back in my pocket / You're sketching my cool," Taylor wails in falsetto, dropping the lulling conceit and kicking listeners in the teeth. "You make me so nasty / Here comes the girl / She's not permitted to see my world, to see my world!"

Taylor had been feeling sick for a number of days, but nobody was connecting the dots: his car, a worn-down 1977 forest-green Mercedes-Benz, was poisoning him.

"Tim said, 'The lady at the BMV is this cute girl. I'm

going to put on my best charm,'" Brainiac guitarist John Schmersal told music writer Leo DeLuca years later. "He was going to try to sweet-talk her into letting him pass an emissions test."

"He opened the trunk and showed us how, from the wheels up into the trunk, it was all rusted out," Schmersal adds. "The exhaust was just going up into the car."

Carbon monoxide.

"Mr. Fingers" feels longer, more impactful, than its 2:59 running time.

After Taylor wails "She's not permitted to see my world" a second time, Brainiac launches back into the song's juicy bridge. This time, though, engineer Jim O'Rourke slices out everything but Taylor's voice, placing it atop the glitch and sway that triggered the song in the first place.

"I confess I'm loving your architecture / Is that why your brother had me arrested?" Taylor, now shouting, spits out. "If you see my puppets and me / You better get inside, get inside!"

Taylor was driving the old Mercedes-Benz he recently had purchased down on Main Street in North Dayton when he lost control.

Police later said Taylor had been overcome by the carbon monoxide fumes that were pouring into the front seat of his vehicle. He likely didn't even feel himself leave the roadway.

Before bursting into flames, Taylor's car careened into two telephone poles and a fire hydrant just four blocks from his home.

5

●

O'Rourke ended the last bridge with a familiar trope: a rapid swell and pop of static, starting in near silence and culminating with the band bursting into the track's last instrumental measures.

The engineer returned to the trick, albeit on a larger scale, on "Ebb's Folly," a composition with Will Oldham on the soundtrack to the 1998 documentary Dutch Harbor. *But it works best on "Mr. Fingers." It's more compressed and intense, somehow more defiant.*

In one brief moment, O'Rourke pares down the band's increasingly evolved Jekyll reliance on electronics into one device, and then allows its more manic, rock-oriented Hyde to come storming out, passing through the eye of a needle like so many unburdened camels.

Taylor then lets out the last words he'd ever record for a Brainiac song: "My fingers are numb from talking too much."

The band steps aside and drummer Tyler Trent smashes out a few measures of the chorus, wonderfully alone.

The song fades out, reprising the glitches and electronic bleeps that first introduced it.

An autopsy later revealed Taylor died from carbon monoxide poisoning. He was twenty-eight.

The song is "Mr. Fingers," the album-closing track on what became Brainiac's swan song, *Electro-Shock for President*. Released on April 1, 1997, less than two months before Taylor's unexpected death, the six-song EP posthumously evolved into the sound of a curtain dropping.

Nearly thirty years later, the way Taylor's uneasy falsetto cuts through an art-damaged chorus, or the racket behind Trent slamming the crash cymbals as Schmersal hammers away on his bright-chartreuse Teisco Delray guitar, still continues to cut with a Dadaist edge to the blade.

Brainiac has not gone silent. And these songs still matter.

Your mind wanders as the needle traces the infinite grooves after the last song, the silent loop near the center of the EP. You hear nothing but static as the record continues to spin.

Then you raise the needle, the mechanical arm, and take the disc off the record player. You carefully return the vinyl and sleeve to its rightful place on the mantel.

When Brainiac's music plays, the band is still alive—even if just for a moment. And then you remember the story.

1. "LIKE DEVO ON ACID"

Brainiac was born, fully formed, in Dayton, Ohio, in the early weeks of 1992.

The quartet quickly drummed up a fair amount of local acclaim, renown even, with its bombastic live sets. They also quickly entered the studio, cutting and releasing a seven-inch single and an impressive debut LP within the group's first year of existence.

Grass Records, the first label to sign Brainiac to a formal deal, released the band's full-length debut, *Smack Bunny Baby*, in July 1993. Any listener within shouting distance must have recognized it as a powerful declaration of intent.

Brainiac had birthed a Martian version of nineties electro-punk driven by quirky alternate tunings and unusual guitar figures, gurgling Moog machines, and more hooks and melodies than any alt-rock band had employed since the Pixies a decade earlier. To paraphrase a commonly used trope: the young band sounded like Devo on acid. Shortly after touring to support *Smack Bunny Baby*, the band split ways with original lead guitarist Michelle Bodine.

Then something wonderful happened.

Brainiac got weirder.

BRAINIAC

The group's second LP for Grass, 1994's *Bonsai Superstar*, and its Touch and Go Records debut, 1996's *Hissing Prigs in Static Couture*, were even more obtuse and calculatedly off-kilter. The songs, many of which surged with an explosive energy, announced themselves as outliers; they were further flung than what had appeared on the group's debut. Guitar-driven choruses with shouted refrains, all too common to nineties alt-rock, were replaced by mutant chords and meandering bits of New Wave–ish guitar, a drummer who pounded away with reckless abandon, and sometimes jagged eruptions of sound.

Taylor, a charismatic front man with an easy smile and piercing, inquisitive eyes, led the group ever forward with aplomb, not so much singing or screaming as acting out song-narratives in a series of peculiar character-voices. He wailed, he muttered, he insinuated. He also cut a mean falsetto.

Tim Taylor during the band's first trip to New York City in 1992. Photo by Michelle Bodine.

Somehow, though, all the weirdo music Brainiac was creating was far from inaccessible. On the contrary. Though Brainiac toyed with jazz and New Wave colors, punk rock energy, and an avant-garde approach to studio experimentation, Taylor still unfurled tons of earwigs and nuanced melodies—both musical and vocal—among Brainiac's sometimes-spastic, often-manic noise-rock delivery. On top of it all, Taylor's frequent deployment of what he called "incidental" noises—a "yeah," an "uh-huh," a "da-da-da-da-da-da"—lent an oddball brand of pop sensibility to the group's attack.

Above all, unlike many of the band's post-punk and post-hardcore contemporaries, Brainiac sounded like they were having a fucking blast. On *Bonsai Superstar*, they distanced themselves from the first LP's brand of fuzzed-out (if a little dissonant) bopsody—for example, the radio-ready staple "Ride." Listeners were introduced to the Bizarro-world guitar figures of new lead guitarist John Schmersal. ("Schmersal would play these chords—you've got to have a master's degree in algebra to know what the hell they are," one music writer told me.)

The new record also happened to illustrate a songwriting prowess far more mature than the band's years. The songs, which toyed, among other devices, with quiet/loud dynamics, were miles removed from the "three-chords-and-a-cloud-of-dust" punk recidivism some bands were peddling in the wake of Nirvana's early nineties rock awakening.

Brainiac's sound did not go unnoticed.

"They were hands down the weirdest and most engaging band I'd seen," wrote Mogwai's Stuart Braithwaite in his

2023 memoir *Spaceships over Glasgow: Mogwai, Mayhem and Misspent Youth.* "Super melodic but incredibly obtuse."

Then came 1997's *Electro-Shock for President*—a placeholder of sorts. A segue, a short but densely packed song cycle that unexpectedly became a sort of epitaph. An indication of what could have been.

Brainiac left indelible fingerprints on the nineties "alternative" scene, then a money-generating giant for a pre-Napster music industry. Legend has it the group's records sold well for a band on an indie label—though nothing remotely close to achieving gold- or platinum-record status—but the group's influence stretched beyond its power as a unit to generate revenue.

The band crisscrossed the faux-formulaic verse/chorus/verse alt-rock of its era with a frenzied musical modus operandi. Brainiac's members didn't electrify their music, they electrocuted it—with Moog flourishes, the trebly scratch of alternately tuned, dueling guitars, and yes, yes, careful attention to its visual presentation. (The band, known for sporting thrift-shop leather jackets, seventies-era shirt collars, and accoutrements like chain-link dog collars and rabbit-fur vests, eventually garnered a "cute band alert" from *Sassy* magazine.)

Alongside Dayton bands the Breeders and Guided by Voices, as well as larger brother-acts like New York City's Girls Against Boys and Chicago's the Jesus Lizard, the group helped contribute to a nationwide alt-rock charge from its rusted-out, post-industrial Midwest base. It was a charge that was fueled by hometown shows in abandoned warehouses as much as it was by aggressively scheduled tours throughout the hinterland—and abroad.

In an era when young bands still angled for a spot on

MTV, Brainiac made highly original music on their own terms.

Just before their big break, as the major labels circled with juicy contracts, it all ended.

But the legend of Brainiac endured.

The American magazine *Variety* called the quartet "the great lost band of the nineties."

"Creative weirdos who developed their own musical language and whose influence continues to pulse through independent music culture today," the *Chicago Reader* opined in 2019.

"By now we all know the story," *CMJ* magazine wrote in 1997. "Stylish Dayton, Ohio, quartet forms. The group mixes some wacky indie-rock elements with some zany manipulation. It's so intense, so mind-blowing and ridiculous that it's brilliant. The group puts out some records and blows shit up."

Or there was the way Charles Bissell of former Brainiac labelmates the Wrens put it to *Pitchfork*: "They were the greatest live band of all time."

Brainiac's five-year run, as well as its familial roots in Dayton, resonates as a uniquely Ohioan story.

The band surely echoes the innovative spirit of its home, a sprawling but still insular metropolitan area that had produced the Wright brothers, fathers of modern aviation, and National Cash Register (NCR), one of the twentieth century's more influential American corporations. More so, Brainiac followed a path cut for it decades earlier by bizarre yet highly influential acts such as Devo and Pere Ubu—both rooted in Ohio cities and the Ohio experience.

In the nineties, the best days for Dayton—a nondescript downtown skyline surrounded by modest homes and boxy warehouses, many of them long abandoned—were behind it. Brainiac didn't care. Its members did nothing but look defiantly into the future.

Brainiac performing at NewSpace in Dayton. Courtesy of Michelle Bodine.

There also was something very Daytonian about the musicians in Brainiac and their oddball dedication to modesty, to being the underdog. There was a highly and dramatically midwestern bent to it all: aspiring and one-of-a-kind band from a broken-down, minor American city makes it big to prove their turf still means something.

At the time, cool bands, both underground and otherwise, made a racket in American metropolises like New York or Los Angeles—hell, even bands who hailed from Seattle or Minneapolis in the eighties and nineties felt like they were operating on the fringes.

But Dayton? In comparison, a city as small—and shrinking—as Dayton felt universes away, like the stardust-coated surface of some distant planet. It was the era after Nirvana blew up the formula for rock success, but one unfolding before the internet—and the use of cell phones and streaming music—supposedly democratized the industry and tried to level the playing field.

In that context, Dayton might as well have been the dark side of the moon.

Brainiac's members, all Ohio-grown, were proud—almost to satirical lengths—about their modest Dayton origins. They promoted it at concerts, on T-shirts, and in interviews with music writers. It was a kind of knowing wink, an homage to their status as artistic outsiders.

"Each region in Ohio has a different crowd," says Ohio-bred music writer Garin Pirnia, who penned a tome on the state's musical "rebels and underdogs" in 2018. "It's obviously affordable to live here and people have basements and we're close to other cities, for touring."

"People are also doing it out of boredom," she laughs. "But Brainiac was ahead of its time."

Tim Krug, a Dayton-based musician who later would play with Brainiac, said the quartet left deep fingerprints on the fabric of his hometown's music scene.

"They had just gained this mythical status," recalls Krug, a multi-instrumentalist whose hair sometimes obscures his eyes while performing live. "They were this untouchable thing. For a long time, if you had a synthesizer in your band, people would be, like, 'Screw you! You're not Brainiac!'"

One must also consider a band like Brainiac bearing the

weight of the history its region had inherited, as well as the heavy mantle of America's Rust Belt.

Brainiac didn't storm Dayton during World War II or the post-war booms in heavy industry and manufacturing, when the ceiling to the city's population appeared impossibly sky-high. Instead, the group came of age in a past-tense Dayton, after a sinking economy had deflated expectations and blighted many neighborhoods. By the time Brainiac entered spaces to drum up crowds, most of the town's warehouses no longer drove business or industry. Like fellow Rust Belt cities such as Buffalo or Pittsburgh or Cleveland in the nineties, Brainiac's hometown was beaten down. No wonder the band sounded so urgent when it came to raising hell.

Brainiac, in turn, burned even brighter as local signifiers of the underdog's might, with the sense that maybe someday soon David might again knock down Goliath. More than a few contemporaries of the group back in the day called Brainiac "the One," that band that somehow would "make it," who would give a kind of validation to its underdog or outsider status. Forget David and Goliath. Think Rocky Balboa.

What really separated Brainiac from a lot of grunge or grunge-adjacent bands looking to become the next Nirvana—beyond the unique presentation, of course—was Taylor's ability to stitch together nuanced pop melodies with sonically adventurous atmospherics and experimental musical devices.

Then, of course, there were Taylor's Moog histrionics, a legacy of Dayton's seventies funk scene. Rumors still circulate about whether washed-up funk musicians from the area stopped performing and simply sold their gear to pawnshops and thrift stores, only for Taylor to come along years later, buy them cheap, and reinvent them.

The otherworldly trills and turns of phrase from Taylor's Moogs and other synths sometimes thrust forward a beat. Three obvious examples were "Vincent Come on Down," "Go Freaks Go," and "Juicy (On a Cadillac)," all of them excellent, even definitive, offerings. Other times, though, the synths painted and chewed the scenery, à la "Pussyfootin'." On the addictive-as-hell "Status: Choke," Taylor waxed topical and enlisted his instruments to imitate the familiar buzzes, blips, and static hiccups of dial-up internet. The technology of the moment now resembles a time capsule, a kind of fossil, an ancient, predigital reference point.

By the time *Electro-Shock for President* rolled around, Brainiac's music was consumed by its electronic conceits. The group, and Taylor, had flown in the orbit of electronic-adjacent indie bands like Trans Am, and outfits such as Tortoise and Stereolab were blurring the lines between organic performance and digitally constructed sound. Brainiac accordingly started supplementing its familiar Moogs—Taylor gained a reputation for reviving the machines like so many of Frankenstein's monsters—with sequencers, drum loops, and wacky effects pedals.

"I think probably Brainiac's big contribution regarding expanding notions of indie and underground rock was that they made synthesizers cool in a world of guitars. With the success of Nirvana, everyone was all about guitars."

That's Jason Pettigrew, a music writer who grew up a county away from Pittsburgh in suburban southwest

Pennsylvania. He left his mark on indie rock as an editor for the influential *Alternative Press*, at one time a glossy-faced magazine championing Brainiac's work in the nineties.

Pettigrew had been living in Cleveland, another beaten-down American city, around 1994. It still was early in his *Alternative Press* tenure when Nicole Blackman, a Grass Records publicist, turned him on to the band.

"Jason, I know what you like," Pettigrew remembers Blackman telling him, "and you've gotta hear this!"

"When you turned these guys loose with synthesizers, it was magnificent, but it wasn't pop music—not in this universe," laughs Pettigrew, who still calls 1996's *Hissing Prigs in Static Couture* his favorite Brainiac LP. "The songs were weird, but you could still dance to them, do your 'white man's overbite' while bobbing your head. In a post-Nirvana landscape, I think they really led the charge: 'If you think synthesizers are lame, you'd better grow the fuck up!'"

Howard Greynolds caught Brainiac early.

The Cleveland native and former Touch and Go Records staffer collects and processes his subtle thoughts on Brainiac pretty simply. "It was fucking weird."

"Even though they were just midwestern guys, they had these rock-star personas," Greynolds told me. "But there was never, like, 'We're going to turn this into a career and be doing this when we're fifty or sixty. Fuck, even at thirty.'"

When Tim Taylor and Juan Monasterio were playing in the Wizbangs, a glam-rock predecessor to Brainiac, the concept of a music "career" sounded somehow alien to them. "We didn't know anybody who had got famous, or even knew anybody who knew anybody," Monasterio laughs.

That alien concept started to sound more and more reasonable, more and more within reach, when Ohio bands like the Breeders started landing major-label deals in the midnineties. Brainiac labelmates the Jesus Lizard, Butthole Surfers, and perhaps most notably, Girls Against Boys, each jumped to the majors, with varying degrees of success.

"It wasn't until the early nineties, when the Afghan Whigs got signed and the Breeders are around, that all those things started to happen," Monasterio says. "All at once, you were, like, 'Oh, maybe you could do this!' But, even then, we were definitely pretty stalwart in the idea of 'You don't wanna sell out!'"

Let it be read into the record: Brainiac never did sell out.

After three increasingly popular and critically well-received LPs, the band's *Electro-Shock for President* EP departed from the script in 1997. Influenced by the harrowing electronics of artists like Throbbing Gristle, the EP sounded the group's—and most definitely Taylor's—new musical direction. It made the case that Brainiac wasn't dumbing down its sometimes jittery but also melody-laden presentation for broader audiences.

Music critics of the time called the EP an early indicator of the band's evolving sound and dropped hints about what Brainiac was cooking up for its forthcoming LP—a possible major-label debut. Brainiac shows swelled with bigger and bigger crowds. The music press fawned over the ascending group.

Then their front man was killed in a violent single-car crash days before the band was set to fly to New York to ink its major-label deal.

In hindsight, *Electro-Shock for President*, an EP that hit streets less than two months before Tim Taylor's death, unwittingly became a symbol for Brainiac's unfulfilled promise, a tumultuous timeline cut short by unanticipated tragedy.

MUSICAL INTERLUDE: "SUPERDUPERSONIC"

*L**et's dance to architecture!*
When Brainiac played live, the band didn't lunge or lurch around only to gradually build up and expand into a manic-paced frenzy. The group simply started off thrashing.

"You should come and see Brainiac because we are mainly a live band," said Taylor in an undated interview with ULTRA *magazine. "It is not easy to capture the intensity we have on a record. Moreover, we mangle our records onstage. We don't play exact duplications of our material. Some people who know us have already told us that they don't even recognize the songs anymore. We don't want to be tied to the arrangements we use on the records . . . we are a live band."*

Few Brainiac songs circa 1992 or 1993 capture the heaving energy of the group's early live performances like "Superdupersonic," the second A-side from the group's proper debut, a seven-inch single cut for Limited Potential Records in 1992. Though recently resurrected for inclusion on one of Brainiac's special Record Store Day releases in 2021, the 2:49 song remains obscure beyond a circle of Brainiac completists. (Good luck finding a trace or hints about its lyrics online.) Its early subtitle—the seemingly relevant "Theme from Brainiac"—

was dropped in '21.

"Superdupersonic," with its hypercharged New Wave refrains and Taylor's rapid-fire leading-man delivery, might be one of the earliest documents to suggest how Brainiac sounded when playing to a live crowd in its first year of existence. If the song is any indication, Brainiac's live-wire electricity would've provided a compelling argument to pay attention, even in the group's nascent stages.

It starts out pretty basic.

After the engine-warming churn of a menacing synth and then carnivalesque bleeps of sound, a kind of foreshadowing, Trent kicks the band into gear—somewhat literally. His backbeat, accented every few measures in the verses by a crash cymbal, borders on early hardcore, a quick, galloping point/counterpoint between snare and kick drum. Bodine and Monasterio, no slackers, waste little time diving into the verses and offer a full-frontal assault in 4/4 time.

Bodine's rapid succession of detuned power chords are driven forward by staccato strumming rhythms that almost suggest a debt to the guitars of seventies funk. Taylor, as always, works hard to steal the show, both with pulsing synths blaring out an alarm and his energetic vocal delivery, which was filtered through at least a couple of distortion pedals.

The Superduperseven *single remains a product of its time. For one, many of Taylor's lyrics, even the incidental noises he'd come to later master, are buried below the surface of the guitar. It's a style, sometimes a lo-fi one necessitated by budget, pioneered by recording engineer Jack Endino and others, and popularized by grunge and punk bands in the late eighties and early nineties. The technique, which must have seemed pretty timely in 1992, almost makes it impossible to understand what Taylor is barking until the choruses.*

And what choruses they are!

After Trent has dug deeper into the band's bottom end with thunder-churning rolls on his floor toms, Brainiac launches into the hook. Taylor, of course, nails the spit-take leads, the sort of energetic thrust of the delivery. The band also overlays a complementary vocal track right on top of it: a dry recording of Taylor, without distortion, repeating the song's title in a lilting, almost Beach Boys–inspired singsong.

There are great details the band would work on to improve later, such as Taylor's faux-sexy voice, flirting with falsetto, that he employs when slyly tossing in closing remarks after the band has stopped making a racket. (We also love that dirgy lone guitar chord Bodine strokes out following the song's denouement.)

Throughout, Brainiac also displays an early adeptness at knowing when to cut to a bridge, instrumental or otherwise. Even early on, these guys didn't waste a lot of time getting to the point.

When performed live, "Superdupersonic" must've sounded like an adventure—not maddening but instead pulse-quickening. No wonder Brainiac adopted the piece as its "theme."

This is music with all the fat cut off. This is no cracked machine.

2. A HISTORY OF BUCKEYES

Tim Taylor's death does not begin or end Brainiac's story. It's just part of a larger narrative rooted deep in the soil of the city that bred it: Dayton, Ohio.

Those who have called Dayton home stretch back far beyond modern Ohioans to the nomadic Paleo-Indians, who arrived there some 12,000 years BCE. Near the end of the Ice Age, also known as the Pleistocene Epoch, mammoth, mastodon, musk ox, and caribou roamed the grassy plains of Ohio.

Eventually, the climate warmed; the Ice Age's glaciers grew helplessly self-conscious and retreated. The Archaic peoples arrived, calling parts of the state home from 8,000 to 1,000 BCE. Then came the Woodland period, which stretched until the early 1200s. Evidence and artifacts suggest the Shawnee, Wyandotte, and Delaware lived and hunted in Dayton long before white European settlers arrived.

Ohio joined the Union on March 1, 1803, and Dayton was incorporated two years later.

By the 1880s, after the national moment of reckoning in the American Civil War, the Industrial Revolution had changed the way people lived and worked in Dayton. In

1917, the government established a sprawling US Air Force base that remains the metropolitan area's largest employer.

Dayton also played an outsized role in the American conversation in the forties and fifties when US officials dedicated millions of dollars to construct the nation's highway system.

Interstate 75 runs north and south across the United States, connecting the southern tip of Florida with the Canadian border in Michigan, a span of well-weathered asphalt 1,800 miles long. Interstate 70, on the other hand, runs east to west, connecting Utah with Baltimore. Today, the interstate passes through multiple cities and metropolitan areas, including Denver, Kansas City, St. Louis, Indianapolis, and Pittsburgh.

Where do these two nation-spanning highways meet? The city once dubbed the "Crossroads of America," of course: Dayton, Ohio. Even American infrastructure had high hopes for the southwestern Ohio city.

In the twentieth century, Ohio left its mark on the world of music, playing an active role in nearly every genre and movement that evolved due to advances in recording technology. In 1937 and 1938, folklorists John, Alan, and Elizabeth Lomax made field recordings in Ohio for the Library of Congress's Archive of American Folk Song.

Jazz flourished in the Buckeye State.

Art Tatum, one of America's most influential jazz pianists, was born in 1909 in Toledo, where he started his professional career and recorded his own radio program while still a teenager—a powerful emblem of Ohio's "can do" work ethic. Cleveland had Freddie Webster, who influenced Miles Davis; Zanesville the ragtime composer Harry Guy; and Springfield the arranger and pianist Charles Thompson. Dayton was no outlier. It counted among its native sons Billy Strayhorn, a close collaborator of jazz icon Duke Ellington.

Dayton, however, really entered the contemporary musical lexicon in the seventies with trendsetting funk bands such as the Ohio Players, Slave, Sun, Faze-O, and Bootsy's Rubber Band.

Ohio Players' keyboardist-vocalist Walter "Junie" Morrison, leading the charge, penned the group's hits in 1971 and 1972—compositions with simple titles, like "Pleasure" and "Pain." In 1977, after producing and releasing a trio of solo LPs to some critical acclaim, Morrison went national and joined George Clinton in Parliament-Funkadelic. With them, he penned "(Not Just) Knee Deep," a number one hit on the R&B charts in 1979, and he figured prominently into at least two P-Funk LPs—*One Nation Under a Groove* and *Motor Booty Affair*, which went platinum and gold, respectively. He was inducted into the Rock & Roll Hall of Fame in 1997.

The most relevant Ohio influences on Brainiac, however, didn't hail from Dayton.

New Wave icons Devo formed in Akron, Ohio, in 1973, though the rambunctious, yellow-suited, red-hatted bunch really dived into the national conversation when they released their hit single, "Whip It," seven years later. Adventurous rock band Pere Ubu, another Brainiac influence, formed in Cleveland in 1975.

In the meantime, Dayton's industry-driven economy started to metamorphize.

Dayton resonated as a post-war boomtown in the fifties

and even into the sixties but took a hit when American investment in heavy industry plummeted a decade later. The second half of the twentieth century was not kind to Dayton, as its industrial bones aged into the definition of what economists call the Rust Belt.

The idea of a "Rust Belt" in the United States concisely encapsulates the deindustrialization, depression, and population loss that wrapped its arms around many smaller American cities. Detroit. Cleveland. Buffalo. Pittsburgh. Trenton, New Jersey. Youngstown, Ohio. Gary, Indiana.

And Dayton.

The Rust Belt region stretches from the American Northeast—New York and Pennsylvania—into Ohio and West Virginia, parts of the regions that remain the beating heart of the Midwest. The Rust Belt stretches even farther, far into Indiana, Michigan, and parts of southern Wisconsin. It traces a postindustrial trail along banks of once-bustling rivers of abandoned steel mills and coal mines, some literally showing the rust that now defines their residents. In some Rust Belt towns and cities, boarded-up homes and Main Street businesses shuttered decades ago outnumber the ones still in use or operating.

Dayton's population peaked at 262,332 in 1960, and its population was halved over the next forty years.

The hits kept coming.

In 2017, Dayton's drug crisis led the National Institutes of Health and others to dub it the Overdose Capital of the US. A year later, Dayton gained the suspect recognition of becoming a highlighted subject of a PBS *Frontline* documentary titled "Left Behind America." The film traced how the once-booming city continues to struggle in a post-recession economy.

This is the environment in which Brainiac was bred: a faltering city with a once-proud heritage.

After Brainiac's initial demise in 1997, Dayton's population continued its downward trend—like Buffalo, like Pittsburgh. Dropping, dropping. It has shrunk 17 percent in terms of residents within the city limits since 2000 alone. Census data shows 98 percent of similarly sized cities in America have grown faster than Dayton in the past two decades. On many days, despite efforts to reinvent commercial spaces and manufacturing buildings as lofts near Dayton's city center, its downtown remains skeletal, a faint suggestion of its former self.

As of 2022, the median household income in Dayton barely broke $40,000. In the same year, one out of every three people who called Dayton home lived in poverty.

Dayton's music scene has remained vibrant despite the economic challenges its musicians, artists, and misfits face. The city and region often have punched above their weight and inspired some residents to look beyond the statistics to find faith and stability in their surroundings. This especially was true as the early commercial internet fanned flames on regional music scenes in the post-Seattle decades.

Brainiac, a regional sensation in the nineties that resonated far outside Dayton's borders, fit right into that theme, the band's drummer Tyler Trent says.

"That's one of the reasons why I love Dayton," he adds

proudly. "It's a very musical town. It's got a huge, long history—you know, the late seventies funk stuff, Guided by Voices and the Breeders, and a hundred other amazing bands no one's ever heard of."

Guitarist John Schmersal was born in Ohio but lived in Vineland, New Jersey—in the southern half of the densely packed state, also known as "Jersey Devil" territory—before moving to a Dayton suburb in middle school. Schmersal thinks indie-rock aficionados—we'll say it for him: hipsters—visiting the southwestern Ohio city won't glean much insight about its musical potency by patronizing city businesses or driving its streets.

"It's a real trip," he jokes. "It's funny because people talk about going to Dayton or whatever and they want to find out why Guided by Voices and the Breeders came from here. I'm like, 'I don't know what you're gonna find. You definitely might get a feel for the gritty aspects of an industrial midwestern city.'"

T-shirt from Limited Potential Records. Courtesy of Michelle Bodine.

Brainiac was proud of its origins, though, and wore its Dayton roots on its sleeve—sometimes literally. "Fuck Y'All, We're from Dayton," read one of their early T-shirts. The group imprinted the phrase on a banner that at one time accompanied them on tour. The same catchphrase now adorns the group's official Facebook page. The phrase became a kind of signifier of midwestern modesty and regionalism—maybe even something more pastoral or inspired.

"You leave southwestern Ohio, and you have people who love Brainiac, of course. But here, it's different," Trent says. "I don't know, there's something about it. I just love it. I love this city. It was a big part of Brainiac."

Tim Anderl, a Dayton-bred contractor and music publicist who later worked for Brainiac, concurs.

"It was incredible to have these completely unique, out-there bands that I, as a young music fan, could latch on to," Anderl says. "There always was this buzz that made them larger than life, like: 'Hey, this is Ohio and we're glad to be here!'"

Trent adds, "We were kind of Dayton superhero representatives everywhere we went."

MUSICAL INTERLUDE: "I, FUZZBOT"

Right from the start, you instantly feel the tension—the gnarling, knot-tightening pull in different directions. This is a band that wants to challenge your notions of how far alt-rock can be reconfigured and stretched. And, yes, they also want you to fucking dance.

As the curtains are pulled open on Brainiac's full-length debut, the entire band jumps to the fore on one collective foot. The noise beckons; a dissonant haze of sound, guitar picks viciously thrumming open strings, is lobbed at the listener. Distorted power chords and open-stringed cacophonies mingle with the crunch of crashing cymbals. It lasts only a few seconds, the new guys churning up the waves and sirens of a musical storm before Trent smacks out a drum fill to count time and the quartet launches into the song's first verse.

The band quickly flashes its hooks.

Original lead guitarist Michelle Bodine's primary guitar riff chugs along like ghost trains plowing down rails, something not entirely out of place for any of the era's grunge-adjacent bands. That is, until the last measure or so. Bodine hits five quick, seemingly detuned, notes, successive figures of sound originating way up the neck of the guitar that suggest something deeper at work. (The five-note reveal of the band's alternate tunings offers all sorts of insinuations and readings.)

"Dull metal eyes / Flaw in my disguise," sings Taylor, his voice slightly adenoidal, as Brainiac deconstructs the verse around him.

Everything surrounding Taylor suddenly feels even more alien. Bodine is offering those quick chops in 4/4 time on the guitar as Trent punctuates each note—falling on the first, third, and fourth measures—by punching the crash or the ride cymbal. But Taylor, interestingly and importantly, provides rhythm by sliding his fingers up and down the frets along the guitar's neck. The technique, which creates a kind of whirly whistle on the high strings, is intended to disorient, perhaps. The very fluid backing, though, also runs as a wispy counterbalance to the defiant, sludgy march Bodine and Monasterio are establishing.

Seeing this live also would have been highly suggestive. The way Taylor must have worked his hands up and down the priapic neck of the guitar to get those notes would've depicted something a little less PG-rated than the lyrical descriptions of robots and such.

"Crosshair stare there / Anywhere mercury flows!" Taylor barks.

The bridge or pre-chorus feels equally dissonant, with both guitars abandoning the grungier verse chords for crescendo-churning high notes, the kind of Eno-ish ambient soar that became de rigueur when deployed by Godspeed You! Black Emperor and Explosions in the Sky years later.

This is weird stuff for 1993.

Then listeners arrive at the chorus, and we begin to understand—from the very first song on their very first LP— how Brainiac was always chasing an unattainable balance between the avant-garde and the anthemic. Pop melodies, no matter how they were dressed or disguised, continually played yin to Brainiac's more aggressive and more daring noise-rock yang.

"Ooh-ooh / Chemical parasite / Speed machine / Combustion engine lies," sings Taylor, his voice sounding smoothed out by production, possibly subtle multitracking. The "ooh-ooh," which is essential to establishing the melody of the chorus, is insanely well done for a band with this much egg still behind their ears.

Now driven forward again by grungy power chords and bopping bass notes, Brainiac dangles the hook in front of the listener—and Taylor and Bodine both deliver on guitar.

"Super shot, hot rod, hate device / You claw and scream and cry," Taylor wails. "Get out of my mind!"

Even from the beginning, Brainiac knew exactly what it was delivering.

3. "JUST KIND OF TOOK OFF FROM THERE"

The members of Brainiac, by allegiance and by birth, were Dayton's sons and daughters—musicians "from" Ohio as much as they were "of" it.

Brainiac front man Tim Taylor, who handled vocal duties for the band and also played guitar, synths, and Moogs, was born at Miami Valley Hospital on July 20, 1968. His sister, Laurie, arrived four years later. The family had deep Dayton roots, with their mother, Linda Taylor, boasting family that moved there from Cincinnati before even she was born. The Taylors continue to live throughout the state.

"I've never really had the desire to move anywhere else," Linda Taylor recently offered.

Terry Taylor, Tim's father, and a professional musician of some renown in his time, arguably became a tremendous early influence on his son, at least in terms of the latter's musical and artistic development. A jazz guitarist and leading man for groups like the Bridge, the Terry & Joe Duo, and later, 'Bout Time, the elder Taylor frequently was out on the road, touring clubs like the Tiger Lounge throughout Ohio and West Virginia.

Taylor's parents separated while he and his sister were

young, and later officially divorced. Terry Taylor lived to see his son die and passed away himself about a decade later, following a battle with cancer.

The younger Taylor showed an interest and aptitude for music even before his first birthday. His mother remembers Tim, still in diapers, singing the words from memory to Peggy Lee's minor hit "You'll Remember Me," off her 1970 LP *Bridge over Troubled Water*. (Linda remembers the house always being filled with "lots of 'easy listening'" and forties pop.)

Taylor's father, seeing the spark of inspiration, bought the boy a drum kit—and weekly drum lessons, so he could read sheet music—at the young age of four. At Orchard Park Elementary School in Kettering, Taylor learned to play the cello and joined the school orchestra. There, he met a young Juan Monasterio, also biding his time on cello.

In high school, Taylor, with his shaggy but striking dark hair growing a little longer, swapped out cello for an upright bass.

The nascent songwriter, who later would go on to develop an electricity-surging-through-the-veins stage presence, was focused intensely on learning to master rock 'n' roll guitar, his mother recalls.

"He just kind of took off from there," she laughs.

Taylor picked up the six-stringed instrument in the eighth or ninth grade and briefly played with the Bridge, one of his father's jazz bands. Listeners can hear a brief, two- or three-second reference—perhaps an homage—to the Bridge's fluid, Wes Montgomery–informed jazz licks about a minute into the Brainiac song "Radio Apeshot." The song appears early on the band's *Bonsai Superstar* in 1994.

Taylor's mother still remembers her son's first show with

the Bridge at the Dayton club Note for Note. Taylor's father stood in the wings, watching his son, "beaming" as he played his first guitar solo, she says.

"Terry knew," Linda Taylor told me. "And Terry was so proud of him."

Taylor's mother also watched Tim develop a deep appreciation—and an eclectic taste—in different forms of music.

"Tim, he'd listen to everything," Linda Taylor admitted, adding that a young Taylor often liked playing classical records while doing his school homework. "He had such an understanding of so many different kinds of music—I was so proud of him."

After Taylor died in 1997, his father approached Schmersal and the other surviving band members.

"Hey, John, you're going to keep going with the band?" he asked, wondering if Brainiac would continue without its lead singer and principal songwriter.

Even the suggestion bordered on the unthinkable.

"We couldn't do that," Trent says.

Bassist Juan Monasterio was the only member of Brainiac born outside Ohio. He entered this mortal coil in Paris on November 12, 1968, to a French mother who curated and helped repair paintings at the Louvre and a Mexican father, a philosophy professor who later worked at the University of Dayton.

Juan became the middle child, following his older brother, Jorge, and preceding his younger sister, Maria. He played the role well. Even years later as a young adult, Monasterio remained more reserved than his peers. His immovable demeanor and the stability that came with it became valuable tools for Brainiac.

Juan Monasterio, on stage at North Carolina club Cat's Cradle. Photo by Chad Pry.

"My parents met in Italy. My dad was working in Italy, and my mom was doing restorations on the catacombs beneath the Vatican. They met on a train," Monasterio says. "[My dad] ended up taking the job in Dayton. So we moved there, and my mom became a French professor at the school as well."

In Dayton, Monasterio said his family was "definitely different" and "kind of interesting."

"My parents didn't really know the rules of American life, so they couldn't really teach you those rules," Monasterio says. "My dad, he bought me this bike that I really liked. And so, I'm driving around. I go drive it over to where the other kids are and they're like, 'That bike you're riding, that's a girl's bike.' It would just be things like that. Or curse words. I would use them incorrectly, and people would make fun of me because I really didn't know what they actually meant, because my parents didn't use them.

"I think it's sort of the beginning of making you feel a little bit different," he adds, "and kind of an outsider."

Monasterio's parents seemed distinctly proud to educate him in the visual arts from a young age. It left an impression. Today, the art school graduate works in California as a designer in the motion graphics field.

American popular music was a much different story. It never quite figured into the picture. "It was kind of a strange thing, because my parents only listened to classical music," Monasterio says. "I remember one time going with my mom to Paris to visit some of her friends. I must have been twelve years old. And then they started showing me all these records. 'Oh, this is a Police record.' I heard *Sgt. Pepper's* when I was twelve years old and thought it was a new record. I was like, 'What is this?! This is the best record I've ever heard!' It was always that kind of thing, where I was just coming at popular culture at weird times."

Around the time of the Paris trip, when he was in fifth or sixth grade, Monasterio met Taylor while the two played cello for the school orchestra.

"I was awful!" Monasterio laughs. "What's strange about it is sometimes I would be first chair—I can't even understand how that could possibly have been the case. But I do remember that."

Monasterio and Taylor became inseparable after high school, both growing to be informed by bands like Sonic Youth, the Pixies, and Pere Ubu. They liked to experiment with music in basement spaces, laying the foundation for the partnership they later chiseled to perfection in Brainiac. Before that, however, they formally joined each other in the Wizbangs, a glam-rock outfit whose sound, if only vaguely, hinted at what was to come.

After Taylor's death, Monasterio went to live in New York City.

"The East Coast is weird—especially back then, it's not so much now—because people used to be so much 'more' on the East Coast than they were in the Midwest," Monasterio said. "I don't know, I spent a fair amount of time in New York City in the late eighties, early nineties and stuff, when New York was still New York. People had New York accents and stuff. I remember it was always very disconcerting to me as an Ohio person."

After living in New York, Monasterio started zigzagging to different locations. He moved to Cabo, Mexico, and later to California. Today, he lives in Santa Monica. But Monasterio—who studied art at the University of Cincinnati, "a good design school," he told me—continues to harbor a soft spot for Ohio.

"I like Midwest people. I think they're the best people," says Monasterio, who looks stockier, if only slightly, and more stoic in his fifties since losing much of his hair. "We used to spend every summer, three months a year, in Mexico City, hanging out with my cousins and stuff. But I always liked Ohio. It just seemed normal. I guess wherever you grow up just seems like the normal place. When we were growing up, it didn't feel like such a small town, that we felt completely off the grid or whatever."

Monasterio adds he couldn't live there today. "That's the thing about the Midwest. If it wasn't for the weather, I could happily live there. But the weather is really the deal-breaker for me."

John Schmersal, the second person to play lead guitar in Brainiac, was born on June 11, 1973, in Toledo, Ohio, the youngest of four children to an electrical engineer and a nurse. The family left Ohio for New Jersey for his dad's job in '77, then moved back to Ohio—specifically to Beavercreek, a suburb nine miles east of downtown Dayton—about ten years later.

Around the sixth grade, he picked up the bass. (He admits he was a huge Police fan before he discovered punk. Others remember him admiring the Cure in high school.) Schmersal remembered his hands were too small at the time for the guitar, which his father and sister both played recreationally. He also toyed with drums. And trumpet.

By the time he was attending Beavercreek High School, Schmersal had switched over to guitar and was playing what he called "a black metal-y Charvel," a domestic brand of electric guitar. He met Tyler Trent, and the two joined Jeremy Frederick in a band awkwardly named Sunken Girraffe. The misspelling was intentional.

Schmersal also started taking in disparate sounds—from John Fahey to Sonic Youth—and religiously read the punk fanzine *Maximumrocknroll*, then in its heyday and at the peak of its underground influence.

Schmersal corresponded with like-minded misfits. In 1989, one friend from Toledo, who played in a band called Jailbait Babysitter, sent Schmersal a cassette tape through the mail. Side A of the tape captured Melvins' seminal *Gluey Porch Treatments*; side B was Nirvana's *Bleach*, the group's full-length debut on Sub Pop. The sounds coming out of the speakers when he listened (and relistened and relistened) to that tape became formative to him as a musician.

Schmersal graduated from high school in 1991—"the year punk broke," a.k.a. the year Nirvana's *Nevermind* kicked "King of Pop" Michael Jackson off the top of the Billboard charts.

(Sidenote: Some members of Brainiac were excited to experience Nirvana's aggressive but hook-laden form of grunge in the flesh before Kurt Cobain became a multimillionaire. Taylor and Monasterio caught the Seattle trio at a basement show in Cincinnati shortly before Geffen released *Nevermind*. There were only thirty or forty people in the crowd.)

Schmersal left Dayton to attend two years of college at Ohio University in Athens, Ohio, studying communications, working in the school's program, and DJing at the college radio station.

Brainiac came calling around the time 1993 defenestrated into 1994, and Schmersal opted to leave OU to return to Dayton and join the band.

Drummer Tyler Trent was born in Kettering, another Dayton suburb, on October 19, 1972.

At the time of Trent's birth, both his parents were working as elementary school teachers in West Carrollton, which sits about seven miles south of downtown Dayton on Route 75.

Trent's mother grew up near Ohio's Amish Country, and his father was from Baileysville, West Virginia, a village about seventy miles outside Pikeville, Kentucky. Today, Pikeville, a small city of just seven thousand people, promotes itself as a kind of regional hub, an economic anchor, in a largely undeveloped corner of the country. (Rumor has it the Deal sisters' family might also have relatives living near Pikeville.)

*Tyler Trent back stage at North Carolina club Cat's Cradle.
Photo by Chad Pry.*

Trent, too, graduated from Beavercreek High School in 1991. He gave community college a whirl for a semester before heading off to work. He joined Brainiac somewhere between February and the early spring of 1992, while taking short-term jobs through a local firm dubbed Manpower.

One job, which lasted about a week, involved cleaning the bumpers and exhaust pipes of Dayton's city buses. In another downtown gig, he swept out U-Haul storage spaces, often encountering local prostitutes plying their trade.

In his early Brainiac days, Trent's head was topped with a nest of dark, almost black hair, which he sometimes half-heartedly parted down the middle and tucked behind his ears. The 2023 version of Trent, a father and religious man who has been sober for more than a decade, is leaner, more refined. Trent wears eyeglasses now, the rectangular kind with well-defined black frames, and his hair is clipped tighter—short on the sides and combed into an erect semi-wave up top.

The budding musicians started groups young. Taylor, the earliest to get bitten by the band bug, joined local rockers Cousin It around age fifteen.

"Tim was in his dad's band, the Bridge, which is the jazz thing, and then he was in a band called Cousin It, which was kind of like a metal cover band in high school," Monasterio remembers.

Groups often lasted long enough to get named and possibly play a few local shows. The guys took early notes (and perhaps inspiration) from the Austin, Texas, scene of the early eighties, where "bands" would "form" simply to come up with an excuse to plaster flyers for imaginary shows on utility poles in town. This is, allegedly, how noise-rock icons Scratch Acid got their start.

Taylor, who showed an early adeptness for writing original music, pinballed between several such outfits in the late eighties and early nineties.

"I think it goes from Cousin It to the Scam," Monasterio says. "After Dance Positive, he was in a band with my roommates, my college roommates, called Tool Shed. And then somewhere in there we'd always talk about being in a band, but . . . it wouldn't even be a real band. It would just be something you would just sort of talk about."

●

Taylor and Monasterio briefly formed a trio with local musician Steve Schmoll, a glam-leaning hair-metal outfit named Pink Lady. The musical adventure lasted all of two months, in part because Schmoll wanted to play with a drum machine; he was a huge fan of Steve Albini's Big Black. (Schmoll had caught Big Black at least once live. He fondly remembers a Squirrel Bait / Big Black show in the early eighties at the Jockey Club in Newport, Kentucky.)

Though Schmoll liked the idea of using a Roland-style timekeeper, he said Taylor didn't want to deal with the primitive programming associated with that. At the time, Pink Lady was using a Commodore PC to do all the drum programming. It was, to make an understatement, a bit laborious.

Pink Lady had written—maybe—three songs, "all of them now lost," Schmoll says. The trio never played a live show.

Schmoll, who today lives and runs a record store in Cincinnati, stuck with Taylor and Monasterio after the Pink Lady breakup. He occasionally would go out on the road with Brainiac—selling T-shirts at merch tables, just helping out. He later became the group's default live-sound engineer.

"I was always complaining about the sound," Schmoll admits. "They were so odd-sounding that the sound people didn't know how to mix them. A lot of times [Tim's synths] wouldn't be in the mix or it would be buried, things like that. At the end of one tour, I kept complaining about the sound and Tim was like, 'Okay, well, next time we go out, you're the sound guy!'"

Schmoll also used his knowledge from having worked at a recording studio to engineer one of Brainiac's first seven-inch singles.

As early Tim Taylor projects go, the Wizbangs lasted a bit longer than its predecessors. The group even released a demo recording on cassette around March or April of 1991—it's still available to hear in electronic form if you do a deep dive online.

Wizbangs flier. Courtesy of Michelle Bodine.

Presentation in the Wizbangs also was key, with each member making sure to dress just right for live shows. By this time, Tim's mop of dark hair crawled past his shoulders and down his back. He often took to donning a rabbit-fur vest. Taylor also started wearing what became a bit of a signature, or fashion shorthand: a metal-chain dog collar around his neck.

Monasterio, who played in the band with Taylor, called the Wizbangs "a great school," in large part because he got to learn the management side of being in a band from local musician Denny Wilson. Wilson previously helped lead the

Dayton group Tooba Blooze.

"They had some kind of success," Monasterio says. "They put out a record on a local label, which is the same one that we ended up putting out our record on. They had toured around and stuff like that."

"He basically showed us this system of how you can make the records and then you send them out," Monasterio adds. "When we quit that band and started Brainiac, that sort of coincided with me graduating from university and I was like, 'Well, if I'm gonna do this, we have to do it because I can't just go out of college and then not do something.'"

Right from the beginning, though, from even before the Wizbangs, Monasterio knew the best thing to do was stick with Taylor.

"I just knew that Tim was special and could make great things," he says. "Day one, I just knew that Tim was going to be famous, one way or the other. Everybody kind of knew it. You'd just meet him, and it was just 'Oh, yeah! He's just one of those people who is operating on a higher level.' So I just said, 'This is cool because now I've sort of attached myself to this thing and I'll get to go along for the ride.' But whether there would have been a Brainiac or not, he just would have ended up in something else. I think it was sort of predetermined."

Other bands whose members played in Dayton in the eighties seemed miles removed from the musicians who formed Brainiac. Monasterio remembers some high school classmates trying to cobble together hip-hop acts.

"They were rapping about Brooklyn, doing Beastie Boys kind of stuff," Monasterio laughs. "And I was like, 'Shouldn't you be rapping about Dayton? Isn't that what rappers do, rap about their neighborhoods and stuff like that?'"

Part of that regional dissonance stuck with Monasterio—and followed him in his late teen years to Cincinnati.

"When I was in art school, I saw a magazine that had that expression, 'Fuck y'all, we're from Texas,'" Monasterio says. "To me, it just shows you how cut off we were from everything. I was just like, 'Oh, I had no idea that was a thing in Texas,' that there were all these T-shirts and things that you could buy there. So I thought, 'That's hilarious! We should do 'Fuck y'all, we're from Dayton!'"

"That sort of became part of our thing: we were from Dayton, Ohio," he says, proudly. "I guess we were always walking the razor's edge of being very pro-Dayton, in terms of who we were and not trying to go away from it. We didn't want to be like, 'Oh, we're actually from the bigger city.'"

Tyler Trent was just nineteen when he auditioned for a spot in Brainiac.

Legend has it the audition might have taken place in or near February 1992. A mutual friend—Frederick, the musician sometimes dubbed "the fifth Brainiac"—handled the introductions. (We have to include this somewhere: Frederick later dated Hole bassist Melissa Auf der Maur, for what it's worth.)

And Trent met Taylor and Monasterio at a dance club in Dayton.

"So they both had hair down to their butts and they're wearing full leather pants, leather jacket—Tim had a rabbit fur vest on," Trent recalls. "It's hilarious. They were still so cool somehow and just intimidating. So we set up a tryout time, I think about a week later or so, and I just lugged my drums down to Tim's basement. And he just started playing me some of the songs, just to familiarize me before I started playing along. That was my first experience with Tim's songwriting. And I just instantly was blown away."

Trent said the group—which also featured lead guitarist Michelle Bodine, a local musician also of some renown—had tried out several other drummers. All duds.

Trent doesn't remember which of Taylor's songs he played along with in that basement. It clearly left an impression. Taylor and Monasterio asked Trent to join the band that same day. "Sure," Trent replied.

He was Brainiac's youngest member; his bandmates crowned him "the Kid."

"The late eighties were a really cool punk rock scene here in Dayton, really great bands," Trent says. "But what Tim was doing just sounded nothing like that. And, of course, that would evolve even more from there. I was kind of freaked out by it, just sitting there in the basement. I'd never heard anything like that."

For Michelle Bodine, the band's first lead guitarist, rock 'n' roll was a family affair.

"This kind of goes way back, but my brother and I started playing guitar at a pretty early age," says Bodine, who today still sports the straight and sandy shoulder-length hair she had at the time of Brainiac's debut. "My dad was in a band—well, lots of bands—and they would practice in our garage. So, we would go out there and play."

Once Bodine secured her driver's license, she'd trek around Dayton to other friends' houses, especially those who played an instrument. The informal jam sessions eventually led to live sets, though few of the early ones paid.

"We would drive around and just kind of look for parties to play at," she laughs. "We would see people partying outside and we would just go and be like, 'Hey, can we play?'

"You'd do stuff like that because you kind of make your own fun in this town—there's not a whole lot to do," Bodine says.

Michelle Bodine on stage at Chilly's in Cincinnati. Courtesy of Michelle Bodine.

In those early years, Bodine started a band with her brother, Scott, that became the Method. Before she knew it, she joined friends in other bands—many of them metal bands—and rented a shared practice space at a spot known colloquially as the Front Street Warehouse. Many Dayton bands can track their origin stories there.

"We started practicing over there and didn't really have a drummer still—I mean, we had one, but he wasn't very reliable," Bodine admits.

Going to shows of her brother's second band, Kill Us,

and others such as Dr. Creep, Bodine often started running into—and eventually developed a friendship with—Tim Taylor. Taylor even played drums with the Bodines in the Method "a couple of times," she remembers.

Scott Bodine, Michelle's brother, likes to joke about the trajectory of the Method, whose later lineup went on to win the Battle of the Bands competition in Dayton in 1991, the year before Brainiac blew up the place.

"The Method, we were quote-unquote 'kind of a big deal,'" he recalls recently.

Both Bodines, in the post-Brainiac years, went on to play together in the alt-rock outfit O'Matic.

The early nineties were an era before cell phones or text messaging, when even using the internet or sending email had not been widely adopted. So Taylor and Bodine talked a lot on landline phones. She was studying classical guitar at Wright State University, a public school near Dayton, and playing alongside three or four other guitarists in a chamber group. Taylor was intrigued and would call Bodine and ask her to put down the phone and play, so he could hear what she was developing for the chamber group. He also turned up in the crowd at a couple of Wright State recitals.

"I think through all that, through him playing drums with that band that I was in and then hearing me play the classical stuff, I think that's kind of what made him think that I could do the stuff that they were thinking about," Bodine recalls. "So, he came to this show that my brother's band was playing and just asked me if I would play with him and Juan."

The unnamed group had no drummer yet—again, this is before Trent arrived. Bodine said it was always a chore lugging her gear into Taylor's "weird basement," which you entered through "this little, tiny doorway that was maybe not even a doorway."

"It might have just been like a cut out of a door," she laughs. "And you'd have to squat and jump down into the basement. It was kind of a pain in the butt to get our equipment down there. It was a weird place."

Bodine left Brainiac near the end of 1993—more on that later—but remained close to the guitarist who replaced her, John Schmersal. Years after Brainiac's members went their separate ways in '97, Schmersal invited Bodine's then-new band, Shesus, to tour with his post-Brainiac group, Enon.

Brainiac officially formed in Dayton in January 1992 in a white-sided, single-family house at 420 Neal Avenue in Dayton's residential Riverdale neighborhood.

The band in 1992: l-to-r, Tim Taylor, Juan Monasterio, Michelle Bodine, Tyler Trent. Photo by J. Fotoman.

Driving down Neal Avenue today, you could pass it

quite easily without taking notice. Though Riverdale hasn't fallen prey to some of the blight in other parts of Dayton, its houses still sort of fade into the background. That runs contrary, of course, to the early noises that oozed from it more than thirty years ago.

Monasterio was fascinated with Taylor's songwriting chops from the get-go.

"I just knew that Tim was special and could make great things," Monasterio says. "When we were making those songs, I don't know if I thought they were going to be hits. But I loved every single song that we were making, you know what I mean?"

Taylor also was amazingly consistent, the bassist remembers. And Monasterio was content to play a supporting role musically. He often refers to himself, dismissively, as the least technically proficient member of the band.

"When he'd bring us a song, I'd be, like, 'This song is great!'" Monasterio says. "Then it was the next song. And it would be great too. Then the next one would be great. So I never had any kind of doubt in the music and in Tim's ability. It was just kind of like, 'OK, he'll just make these songs and I'll just do this part and then, as long as we have good people, we'll be able to be in this band.'"

Dayton musician Scott Bodine remembers hanging out in a random basement at one of the first Brainiac practices where Trent played the drums. He doesn't think the group had chosen to use the name Brainiac yet.

Taylor excitedly walked Scott through the just-formed band's proposed sound, particularly the alternate tunings he wanted to employ to set the right tone for its two guitarists.

This guitar here, all its strings are tuned to a D7, Taylor would tell him. And this one over here is tuned to A7.

"I just thought to myself, 'This is ridiculous,'" Scott Bodine laughs. "That guy was a serious lesson in music, a genius in every aspect. And some of the songs, they were immediate. It seems like Tim had everything together and already formed."

Scott's band, the Method, had won the local music competition at Canal Street Tavern in '91, a year before Brainiac took home the Dayton crown. He remembered hearing Brainiac, amid many handfuls of half-assed Grateful Dead cover bands, play live at the 1992 competition.

Tim Taylor on stage at Canal Street Tavern. Courtesy of Michelle Bodine.

VHS footage from some of the performances—you can find it on YouTube—show Taylor playing Canal Street in

'92 as he headbangs or thrashes about onstage, his shoulder-length hair swaying in time to a handful of songs, some of them from *Smack Bunny Baby*. There's not a Moog in sight. But Taylor is clearly in control of the audience.

"They just got it together immediately—I was blown away," Scott says. "Tim was obviously the director. But everybody contributed their own thing. And their sound? I remember it being immediately there."

The group played its first show at the Rathskeller, an "activity space" in the Student Union building at Wright State, on March 12, 1992. The set was short, though a list of what the group played has been lost to time. At the time, the foursome had not yet been christened Brainiac. They appeared in promotional material for the show under the name We'll Eat Anything. Monasterio remembers that the group also briefly had operated under the moniker the Girl Who Met Ozzy.

"I'm surprised how many people say that they were at that first show, because we didn't really even advertise it that much," Michelle Bodine says. "We just wanted to play out, and a bunch of people showed up."

By the time the band opened for touring act Lungfish at NewSpace in Dayton a month later, their name had morphed into Brainiac, a reference to the comic-book character and alien, often green-skinned, who ruthlessly chooses to do battle with Superman.

Sometime after Brainiac formed—specific dates get fuzzy after being stored in the human brain for thirty years—Taylor started to rent a place on North Main Street. He lived there for about four years; his rent started at a modest hundred dollars a month. The Dayton residence became "the Brainiac house." (There are rumors, unconfirmed, of "an infamous Marilyn Manson party." The surviving band members have kept mum.)

In the early months of Brainiac, the group played frequently in Ohio—first in Cincinnati, then over to Columbus.

Brainiac on stage at Chilly's in Cincinnati. Courtesy of Michelle Bodine.

The quartet instantly started playing more and more at area bars, and sometimes at parties held in abandoned warehouses. Though the group were regulars at spots like NewSpace, they also lit up warehouses in Cincinnati, as Rust Belt promoters found new, unique uses for the vacant industrial spaces. As the group's live show improved—and the chemistry between the band members tightened—Brainiac started venturing further and further astray from Dayton.

That was pretty intentional, according to Monasterio.

"Right from the beginning, we could kind of see that local bands would get sort of popular and they'd play week after week in Dayton," he says. "We were like, 'We're not going to do that.' Brainiac played a couple of times a year in Dayton. But we didn't do what other bands were doing, where they were playing, minimum, once a month, just trying to rake it in or whatever.

"We were much more focused on touring and getting out of town, and I think it really paid off," he adds. "Tim was, during that time, just writing a lot of music. I can't remember how many times we practiced each week, but it was probably at least twice, which is a lot, maybe three times a week."

Brainiac's early mode of transport to shows outside their hometown was what several people, including band members like Bodine, called "the terrible van."

Brainiac on tour in "the terrible van." Courtesy of Michelle Bodine.

"It was this yellow van and Tim built a loft in it—and every time we got out of it, we were all blowing black shit out of our noses," Bodine laughs. "We were like, 'This van sucks!'"

Bought by one of Dayton's local concert promoters to encourage local bands to hit the road, "the terrible van" more than served its purpose, albeit with a good measure of ugliness. The promoter, though, had a catch. His personally selected driver, Frank, had to accompany the group and drive the van at all times.

Maybe Frederick wasn't the only "fifth Brainiac" after all.

Steve Schmoll, who played alongside Taylor and Monasterio in the trio Pink Lady, caught his old collaborators' new band early in its tenure. His memory suggests it probably took place sometime in 1992, likely at the Cincinnati venue Shorty's.

"I was blown away—it was just weird to see your friends sound like that, you know what I mean?" says Schmoll, chuckling as he admitted he bore "some low expectations" due to Taylor's and Monasterio's work in their previous trio.

"Seeing them, I was like, 'Wow, this is just mind-blowing!' To see something that good and you can already hear the originality? It didn't sound like anything else. You go and see your friend's band and it's kind of part of you. 'I wanna see what they're doing.' But part of it's 'Oh, I'm doing the friends a favor by seeing them.' And then it ends up being like, 'WHOA!'"

The shows, at first, were similar to a lot of punk and post-Nirvana grunge wannabes of the time. Trent, a Mac McNeilly–style timekeeper who was a step or two above the caveman-smash style of punk drumming, was always highly animated, while Monasterio was more restrained. Before Taylor stepped up to his Moogs, though, he worked primarily behind a guitar, cutting the proto-typical early nineties grunge moves.

Bodine remembers, one day, the switch just flipped. At an early practice, Taylor's penchant for the more colorful, the more bizarre, entered the landscape.

"One day he just said, 'What do you think about keyboards?'" Bodine remembers. "And I was like, 'Keyboards?!' He said, 'Yeah!' And I was like, 'Well, like a Devo-style, New Wave kind of style? Or kinda like a Deep Purple kind of style?'"

"Then, the next time we practiced, he had a keyboard and it was that Realistic one he got from the thrift store," Bodine adds. "It was funny, because at practice he would just start jumping around and stuff. You know, he didn't do that in the beginning. I think he wanted to learn how to jump around and be crazy or whatever."

Taylor later told an interviewer, around 1996 or 1997, how Brainiac's flirtation with Moogs started. He was attending a random party with Monasterio, where the David Bowie song "She Shook Me Cold" started to play. The pair was struck immediately with how cool the Moog sounded filling in for the bass parts in the song.

"We knew a pawnshop in town had a Moog, so we went to see if we could buy it," Taylor told the writer. "The thing had probably been sitting there since the seventies, and the owner didn't understand why we wanted it. He said, 'You know, it's not MIDI-compatible—it's useless!' So we bought it and came back the next day and picked up another Moog Rogue, a Moog Prodigy, and an ARP Odyssey as a package deal for a hundred bucks.

"They sounded cool, but nobody in the group wanted to play the Moogs," Taylor laughed. "So it fell to me by default."

MUSICAL INTERLUDE: "SEXUAL FRUSTRATION"

We all have internalized the refrain. It lives on as one of Tim Taylor's most iconic—and surely most quoted— lyrics. And it absolutely drives the claws of one of the band's best songs deep into a listener's cerebellum.

"Boom sha-locka-locka—ooh, I think she likes me!"

"Sexual Frustration" falls eight tracks into 1994's Bonsai Superstar, *but it has become the LP's lynchpin, the accumulation of many of its finest factors. The song, just three minutes long, starts with the illusion of low fidelity—a musical aperitif. Taylor sensually croons out incidental noises (you can almost imagine his upper lip curling in an Elvis-style snarl) that then are filtered through some sort of mutant machine—part bullhorn, part shortwave radio.*

One wail, ascending, leads into a quick cut—a nondiegetic edit. Trent enters, his simple drumbeat, which echoes the surf-rock beats of the 1960s, runs through layers of musical lint and fuzz. Detritus!

Brainiac then launches into the song's first verse, Schmersal offering a sparky guitar figure on each downstroke.

Brainiac sometimes concocted its best moments when it deconstructed a song, carving down each little element into its most vital or invigorating form. Throughout the canon, we repeatedly hear Trent and Monasterio, the band's sense of time and volume, working on a different wavelength, a different sense of colors, than Taylor's and Schmersal's guitars, or Taylor's synths. Each band member would stay locked into the same time signature—this isn't the interwoven basses and guitars of midnineties post-rock. But Brainiac's lead and rhythm guitar often strayed from each other or offered complementing parts, especially as the group matured as songwriters.

Not on "Sexual Frustration."

The entire band starts together quickly, pouncing on the first beat, then giving a double punch before the third beat: boom, POP-POP! During the bridges, Taylor helps emphasize the coupled beats by delivering two rhythm-accenting notes on the synth, little blasts, or shards of white noise: boom, POP-POP!

It's hard to hear what Taylor is saying during the verses. "I've got my hand stuffed into my suit," he offers at one point. And, "So remember that I don't take dares." Even internet sleuths offer question marks in deep readings of this song's lyrics.

The synths feel pretty aggressive on this one, pulsing out musical references to fifties-era sci-fi films in a couple bridges. It sounds as if the listener is being confronted at times by the business end of a phaser gun. And Taylor keeps barking out the lyrics. What listeners can pull from the narrative is highly suggestive—and that might be the point. (He definitely drops a callout to masturbation at least once.)

"They got my testimony on a lie detector," Taylor moans. "Broke the needle so they're setting me free!"

Then, as we meander forward, Taylor announces his orders: "I think I found a cure for my sexual frustration!"

The second chorus, all hooks, is absolutely killer stuff—a little more broken down and chiseled into a fine-point earworm than the first go-round. As on the opening, Taylor croons his lyrics over Trent's driving beat.

"Boom sha-locka-locka—ooh, I think she likes me!"

4. "RIDE YOURSELF AWAY, EACH AND EVERY DAY"

Brainiac, before even entering the recording studio, had quickly gained its live-show sea legs.

While the group continued wowing local audiences at Dayton venues, it played one of its first out-of-town gigs—opening for esteemed Chicago acts the Jesus Lizard and Tar, no less—at Sudsy Malone's in Cincinnati on August 6, 1992. Again, no full setlist survived, but those who caught early Brainiac shows remembered their performances at Sudsy Malone's being high-octane ones, always memorable. (YouTubers looking to tunnel down the rabbit hole can spot video online of the band's February 1997 show there.)

Despite the occasional touring band passing through southwestern Ohio, where Brainiac sometimes played supporting roles, the group continued to rely on salt-of-the-earth shows, such as ones staged at the Palace Club. That venue surprisingly was visited by the likes of Steve Albini as he passed through Dayton. Essentially, it was a hole-in-the-wall at a Beavercreek strip mall, a space you easily could mistake for a vacant bodega. (If it was good enough for Shellac and Sebadoh, though, it was good enough for Brainiac.)

Monasterio, beginning to form his role as a sort of band manager, started contacting labels and sending through the mail scores of basement-recorded demo tapes, then de rigueur. In hindsight, they were very lo-fi, even crude, but they got across the point.

Some attempts hit, some didn't.

With Limited Potential Records, which always has been associated with the band's "Fuck Y'All, We're from Dayton" T-shirt, the outreach hit. The band officially debuted on a commercial recording in the autumn of 1992 when Limited Potential released a Brainiac seven-inch EP, *Superduperseven*. The cover hinted at the Brainiac logo—the lowercased, italicized b offset in a kind of cloud or bubble—the group would continue to use for years. (Like we said, these guys were born fully formed.)

The songs on *Superduperseven* were familiar to those who had been following the band's live-set trajectory. The A-side opens with the pop-influenced drive, no pun intended, of "Ride," at that point one of the group's most accessible songs. (The song's close, where Taylor continues to sing "Ride yourself away, each and every day" ad infinitum is way, way too inviting to sing repeatedly over and over again in the shower.)

Remember, though, Brainiac always was balancing its poppier sensibilities with tracks that displayed a more adventurous, often manic-paced, timbre. Enter the second song on the A-side: "Superdupersonic (Theme from Brainiac)." Taylor still employs a little poppy, singsong edge to his backing track, yes, yes. But the delivery that drives the song, on the contrary, is 100 percent Devo on ephedrine, with all the pulse-heightening pleasure and increased blood pressure that comes with it. (Insert reference here on how mentioning ephedrine or speed use while describing Brainiac is highly apropos.)

Taylor's synth flutters over an aggressive, borderline-hardcore drum pattern from Trent. Bodine's lightning-fast guitar refrains sound less concerned with melody than velocity. They're karate chops to the head.

The song "Superdupersonic," from which the band borrowed the name for its first release, never appeared on a Brainiac LP. Well, technically it didn't. The song finally did appear on the Record Store Day special release *From Dayton Ohio*, which Touch and Go Records put out in 2021. (On that 2xLP, it again appeared next to "Ride." This time, though, that radio-ready nugget followed it. Early favorite "Still Insane" preceded it.)

The first EP's B-side entirely was consumed by "Simon Says." Though early takes on that song are great, the definitive version remains the one engineer Dave Doughman recorded on magnetic tape at Cyberteknics in Dayton. That version—produced or, as the liner notes put it, "decoded" by Kim Deal—appeared only on the CD version of the *Internationale* EP, TG-148, which Touch and Go released in 1995.

The *Superduperseven* EP was a huge step for the band, and Limited Potential was no small potatoes to an ascending indie band like Brainiac. In 1990, the Chicago-based label had released the "I Am One" single, the first release by a then-unknown band named Smashing Pumpkins. Original copies of that seven-inch, which had a limited run of 1,500 copies, today fetch north of $300 through online auctions. Rumor has it that three "test pressings" of the single remain—two owned by Smashing Pumpkins front man Billy Corgan and one by label owner Mike Potential. The label also trafficked music with the likes of the Poster Children, an indie-rock band formed around 1987 at an Illinois college.

(Sidenote: Internet sleuths can find an audio recording on the internet of Corgan getting crochety, with expletives, on a Limited Potential Records answering machine, circa 1992.)

Once Brainiac started to appear on official releases—and not, given one legendary example, handcrafted cassette-tape demos with covers featuring old golfers cloaked in primary colors—they got a taste of their larger potential. (Okay, pun intended that time.) A split single featuring live recordings with riot grrl act Bratmobile, then billed as the Bratmobile, followed close to the end of the year. 12X12 Records, which sometimes was styled as Twelve-Vex-Twelve, did the honors.

On some nights in 1992 and 1993, Brainiac experienced huge success and lots of positive feedback when performing; on others, they drew smaller crowds at unknown haunts. One week, on a Thursday night, Trent remembers the members of Brainiac taking an exhausting, five-hour ride to Chicago to play to a sold-out crowd of more than four hundred avid fans at the Empty Bottle. The next night, a Friday, Brainiac played at a street festival in a faux-Ukrainian village near Chicago's Wicker Park. Just six people stood in the crowd.

Early on, Brainiac also played hometown shows—they tried to keep them to a minimum—at warehouses in East Dayton, a depressed, post-industrial chunk of the city often plagued by crime.

"If you wanted speed or crank or meth, you went there," Trent laughs.

"The warehouse scene in the late eighties, early nineties, though, it was just so cool, just having these hundreds of people in these disgusting, dirty, standing-water warehouses," he continues. "Terrible sound. Four-dollar cover. But there was an electricity there that just was indescribable, and we just wanted to be a part of it."

The warehouses still stand in Dayton today—blocky and bland buildings covered in aluminum siding. Sometimes, in older neighborhoods, Daytonians convened around more distinct ones, ones sometimes stretching up a few stories, set in aging red brick.

Whenever one warehouse show got shut down by the authorities, Dayton bands simply would find a new space where they could play shows or practice without anyone bothering them. In fact, that's how the venue NewSpace earned its name.

Taylor was maturing as a performer with each show, his bandmates remembered, developing his stage presence on tour, his shtick. Bodine quipped that the front man's occasional "dancing" on stage looked "like an electrocuted butterfly."

"He was always saying funny stuff onstage," Bodine remembers. "He'd say it real fast, then he'd start playing. And I'd be there, trying not to laugh!"

Linda Taylor admits the sounds Brainiac was making, at least initially, took her a bit by surprise. "It took me a lot of listening to start to get what Tim was doing with Brainiac," she admits. "But the more I listened, the more I thought, 'Some of this is really brilliant!'"

"We try to make our music sound as original as possible—originality is more important than actually writing songs," Taylor said in an undated interview with *ULTRA* magazine. "I don't think we have a specific style, type of music, or sound. That is reflected in the stuff we use. We play real instruments, we use tapes and synthesizers, and we put a lot of effects on all of that. All this results in very dissonant music. The most important thing is that the music must be original and interesting."

Camille Sciara started her music career at a plainly named New York record store—Record World.

She climbed up the ladder at the shop to management.

Then she got bored.

Dutch East India Trading, not the similarly named outfit stretching back hundreds of years in Europe, distributed independent music, though it gained much of its street cred for its domestic releases of Peel Sessions. It also operated the once-iconic Homestead Records, which was birthed in 1983 and released seminal indie-rock LPs like Sonic Youth's *Bad Moon Rising* (1985) and Big Black's *Atomizer* (1986). That label became the first to put Bad Brains on vinyl in the US, in 1990.

Then Sciara's timeline and the history of Dutch East India became intertwined.

The former music-store manager joined the company in sales, then eventually jumped into a buyer position. While in the latter post, a friend of a friend of a friend (or something like that) handed Sciara a demo by the Toadies on a cassette. She formed Grass Records in New York City in 1993 to release it.

Sciara went on to sign the Wrens, as well as punk outfit Liquid Bike, Dayton band a Ten O'Clock Scholar, and Brainiac, among others.

"Since I had never run a label before, I was going purely on how much I liked what they submitted," said Sciara in an interview with *Trout Fishing in Music*. "Obviously not the best business model for running a label, but for the money we offered it worked to some respect."

In an interview from a few years ago, Bodine said Sciara "was super excited" about Brainiac and inked a two-record deal with them, with an option for a third LP. Nobody has disclosed the financial terms of the agreement. Bodine says the band maintained "total creative freedom."

The label's relationship with Bodine continued after she left Brainiac. Grass Records released *Dog Years*, the first record from Bodine's band O-Matic, in 1996. Grass didn't last long. Music executive Alan Meltzer acquired the company in the second half of the nineties and made a deal with BMG, mutating the label into Wind-up in March 1997.

"If Tim hadn't passed, I'm pretty sure they'd have been the biggest [band on the label]," Sciara says.

With record contract in hand, Brainiac reached out in the winter of 1992 to Eli Janney, an engineer who played in post-hardcore group Girls Against Boys.

The New Yorker—by way of Washington, DC—today leads the house band on *Late Night with Seth Meyers*. Back in 1992, he developed into one of Brainiac's biggest champions, recording all three of their full-length LPs and even name-dropping them to Touch and Go head Corey Rusk. More on that later.

Janney still remembers when the band—"this group of nerds from Dayton"—sent him a lo-fi cassette tape of some material they had recorded on their own. The group, then still with Bodine on lead guitar, worked out the details to record at Brooklyn's Excello Recording as 1992 bled out. The "group of nerds" trekked from Ohio to New York and stayed with Janney and his bandmates at a South Williamsburg warehouse where Janney was living at that time.

"It was always an adventure with those fucking guys," Janney laughs.

Janney had left his mark on New York already by 1993. He played a lot of live sets as a member of Girls Against Boys, then just starting its tenure as a group signed to Touch and Go. He also took various music and production gigs, such as writing the theme song for the MTV show from the NYC-bred, sometimes-Dada-inspired comedy troupe, the State. (The fact that at the time he was dating State member Kerri Kenney-Silver, later a comedic lead in *Reno 911!*, didn't hurt.)

Taylor told a zine back in 1994 that he felt a kinship with Janney, who played synths in Girls Against Boys. He also touted Janney's indie credibility. Taylor was impressed he'd worked with Nation of Ulysses, among others.

"He knows punk rock," said Taylor in an issue of *If You Have Scene, What We Have Zine!*, which was based in Green Bay, Wisconsin. "We're not the most studio-minded band around. If we go into a studio with someone who doesn't really understand our music, we get crushed."

The prospect of working with Brainiac always excited

Janney.

"After doing the three records with them, I got to really see how Tim had a very strong vision of what he wanted to achieve," he told me during a phone interview. "I think it was just a good match because I just wanted to make weird, very intense records."

Girls Against Boys guitarist-vocalist Scott McCloud remembered Janney first getting his hands on the Brainiac tape through the mail.

"The demo sounded completely unhinged in the coolest of ways, a sort of dense explosion of ideas," McCloud quips. "I remember Eli trying to figure out the recording budget and finding the right studio. And being very excited by the outcome."

Grass Records released *Smack Bunny Baby* in July 1993.

The record bore some of the marks of the era, particularly a focus on grungy verse/chorus/verse rock, which was epitomized in tracks like "I, Fuzzbot" and "Ride," which has more hooks than a tackle box. The band's ability to employ quiet/loud dynamics, though in an early stage, is there too: on "Brat Girl," with its Moog refrains; "Anesthetize," a raucous track where Monasterio's pouncing bass takes center stage; and the driving earworms of "I Could Own You," where Bodine's punctuating guitar interjections sound better than ever. On album closer "Get Away," the band's dueling guitars create a surprisingly grandiose sense of scope.

Brainiac's early experimental tendencies also are on display on *Smack Bunny Baby*. Tracks like "Draag" pack their most menacing punch when Taylor plays the role of singer unconventionally and manipulates his voice, with Janney's help, with effects pedals to masterful effect. On "Cultural Zero," Taylor accents Bodine's punchy downstrokes with alarm-sounding Moog side effects, some timed with his roars, a device that disorients the listener. Something even weirder happens on "Martian Dance Invasion": Taylor yields the vocal lead to Bodine, a trick the band would never revisit.

The vinyl version of the band's debut features a bonus track, "Velveteen," which sometimes is credited as "Velveteen Freak Scene." Lore has it an unknown number of the records were pressed on a kind of turquoise- or cyan-colored vinyl. Clocking in at 36:07 (39:54, if you count the vinyl-only track "Velveteen"), the LP's manic, almost rambunctious brand of electro-punk practically breezed past listeners.

Grass Records, fanning the flames on the Brainiac fan blaze, released a promotional seven-inch single—"Smack Bunny Baby" b/w "Hands of the Genius"—after the band released its first EP on Touch and Go in 1995.

The group's debut full-length record introduced Brainiac to a much, much wider audience—and left an impression.

Spin magazine named *Smack Bunny Baby* in its "10 Best Albums of the Year You Didn't Hear" in 1993, comparing the act to Sonic Youth—no small praise. The LP, their writers noted, was "a noisy little devil that benefits greatly from a fondness for Moog synth and a good ear for . . . melody."

"Pure punk exuberance!" shouted AllMusic.

"The best tracks . . . cleverly deconstruct early new wave, using what the band likes, discarding the rest and adding its own innovative ideas to the process," wrote *Trouser Press*, who also raved about Brainiac's "arty approach" and "menacing playfulness."

Smack Bunny Baby, despite its early successes and some

critical raves, went out of print years ago. Copyright issues due to Grass Records' acquisition kept reprints or rereleases off the market for the better part of decades.

Craft Recordings, however, gave *Smack Bunny Baby* the thirtieth anniversary reissue treatment. The label, which works with artists as wide-ranging as Joan Baez, Nine Inch Nails, and Otis Redding, rereleased Brainiac's full-length debut in December 2023, with the label offering an emerald-colored vinyl variant to its online clients. The former vinyl-only track is here again, this time credited as "Velveteen Freak Scene." It's also the first time *Smack Bunny Baby* has been available to stream on services like Spotify.

Similar plans, all unconfirmed, might or might not be in the works to reissue *Bonsai Superstar*.

Janney argues that *Smack Bunny Baby* was the first recording that documented Taylor's push-pull between crazed experimentation and pop accessibility.

"Tim really was the driving force behind a lot of those weirdo sounds [on the album]," Janney admits. "We would just do weird things that weren't really 'correct' in the studio. Like, 'What happens if we just plug this into a mic preamp, then just turn the mic preamp as high as it will go?' We just made these weird, fucking blistering sounds. 'Oh, that sounds so wrong!' And it was like, 'This is great!'

"At its core, Tim was writing these almost weird but very catchy—I wouldn't say poppy songs, but they did have a lot of hooks in them, both vocally and melodically," he adds. "Then he would just douse them in all this craziness on top of it or use weird things to make those melodies."

BRAINIAC

●

By the end of 1993, the band had toured extensively for a unit with such a short history.

Brainiac played that autumn in Louisville with hometown post-rock legends Rodan, then working on the material that would appear on their own debut, 1994's *Rusty*. Brainiac also toured throughout the West Coast—making stops in San Diego, Sacramento, and San Francisco, as well as in Albuquerque, New Mexico—with the Jesus Lizard and Girls Against Boys.

A day before Halloween in 1993, the group helped pack the venue Metro in Chicago—no small feat. (Girls Against Boys and Sugarsmack clearly helped.) A few days later they joined Girls Against Boys, Jawbox, and Poster Children for a set at Irving Plaza in New York City.

As the group continued to tour, though, tensions arose.

Even today, the band members don't remember the source of the problems. Michelle Bodine confronted the topic when being interviewed for the 2019 feature-length documentary about the band, *Transmissions After Zero*.

"I really agonized over what to say for that [documentary]," Bodine admits. "Now, of course, I'm not happy with what I said. Mostly it was a lack of communication with all of us. We're all to blame for it. I was actually thinking, 'I probably should quit my job,' because it seemed like it was getting more serious, and my job was getting more mad every time I would get back and we'd have to leave again."

Bodine was working for a wholesale sporting goods distributor—pitching hunting and fishing gear, camping goods, and so on. She'd handle the design work for their catalogs, each of which stretched beyond seven hundred pages.

"It was starting to get stressful, and I was like, 'I think I'm going to have to quit this [sporting goods company],'" Bodine says. "I was going to talk to them about it, but they started acting kind of weird on the last tour. But there was nothing really said about, 'What are you thinking here? What do you want to do?' It was nothing like that. And I should have brought it up."

"It was, 'I don't understand really what's going on,' but I think they were just getting tired of me having to be tied down to this job, and maybe they just thought I wasn't being serious or something," she adds. "I don't know."

The band members continue to be vague about the details of Bodine's departure. Taylor might or might not have had a conversation with her. And she might or might not have agreed to step down from her spot.

Trent laughs when asked about the documentary's technique to illustrate the change in Brainiac's lineup: a fade to black.

"That's a dramatic thing," Trent offers. "When we decided that was going to be the case, I just hid for, like, two months. I didn't go anywhere. I was scared to death to see anybody because Michelle was so loved—and rightfully so. I, just like a coward, hunkered down until the storm passed."

Then John Schmersal entered the frame.

He was studying at Ohio University in Athens, Ohio. His life, to date, had been typical.

In high school, Schmersal had sold candy "for church"—and, more importantly, for a profit—until about age sixteen.

He worked at OddLots in Beavercreek. During his junior year in high school, he worked in a nursing home. He also was "a Subway sandwich artist" and served on the staff at Sea World in Aurora, Ohio, once the home of Stone Temple Pilots' Scott Weiland.

Schmersal started to snatch up gear with "a sizable amount of that money" from his day jobs. He bought a Music Man HD-130 half tube, an Ampeg cabinet, and several guitars beyond his Teisco Del Ray, which he re-fretted. He developed a penchant for Japanese guitars, lipstick pickups, and instruments from Silvertone and Danelectro. He was not, and is not, a Fender guy. He also collected all sorts of "toy gadgets," including items such as beepers and pagers, to use to strum his guitar, in place of a pick.

Musically, Schmersal had already developed a reputation for flashing a lot of technical ingenuity.

John Schmersal backstage at Cat's Cradle. Photo by Chad Pry.

"I knew all about what was happening with them and all that," says Schmersal, who—remember, remember—had played in Sunken Girraffe with Trent and Frederick back in high school. "Other guys I played with were really into the New York downtown sound or experimental, post-no-wave stuff. So, when I joined Brainiac, I already had like three or four tunings that I was playing in. It was perfect because [Taylor] gave me the structure that I badly needed. Luckily, also, without being in school, I could just immerse myself in that band."

Taylor had mailed a letter to the house where Schmersal was living while studying at Ohio University. The letter sounded pretty simple. "He asked me if I wanted to be in the band, basically," Schmersal says.

Schmersal remembers that Jeremy Frederick, his former bandmate, told Taylor the quirky guitarist would be "the perfect fit for the band." He and Trent, about five years younger than Taylor and Monasterio, also brought something different to Brainiac in terms of their musical influences.

"I think they admired that we were more into the punk and alternative music of the time," Schmersal says. "Tim came from the jazz background and liked more seventies rock. I think [Tim] was maybe attracted to what I could bring to the table."

"I was a total nut job, trying to be Harry Partch Jr."

That's Schmersal again.

Brainiac's new lead guitarist was fascinated with how Taylor had developed his own timbre within the alternate tunings he used to write his songs. He could tell right off the bat that Taylor was incredibly talented at cooking up "novelties" within each song and discovered "eccentricities within the tunings."

In a rare 1997 interview in the United Kingdom, Taylor explained how he cooked up that guitar sound. In short: he tuned a third of the guitar's strings up.

The first two low strings were tuned to E and A, just as in conventional tuning. Taylor would tune his third string, a D, up to E, then his fourth string up to B-flat. The final two strings again follow standard tuning: B and then E.

"So, it's E, A, E, B♭, B, E, but the B♭ will sometimes go up to B or down to A for me," Taylor said. "John sometimes tunes high E down to D, I think. Sometimes I tune my middle E and B♭ down to D for 'I Could Own You.' But we don't do that much anymore because that's too much re-tuning."

Schmersal said "the tunings made perfect sense" to him when he started playing alongside Taylor.

"[Taylor] just gave me the keys to Brainiac, and I understood it immediately," he says. "If I didn't turn out to be a good fit, then, you know, I guess I would just be a weirdo."

By 1994, Brainiac already had some serious touring chops and a full-length record under their belt.

"You tour, tour, tour," Schmersal says. "And so, they were still kind of touring on that first record, so to speak. They had done a ton of touring."

Within months of Schmersal joining Brainiac, the new guitarist had learned the majority of his parts and was helping to write new material. He also had recorded—with former Pink Lady member Steve Schmoll riding the faders, no less—a song with the group, "Dexatrim." Simple

Solution Records released that song in January 1994 as the A-side of a split single with the band Lazy.

For the record, though, the first piece of music Schmersal composed for the band was the screeching mic-on-amp "solo" on "Meathook Manicure."

"It was the first thing that I wrote that [Taylor] really connected with, that he was like, 'That's good!'" Schmersal proudly recalls. "That four-track [recording] ended up getting elevated on *Bonsai Superstar*. It's just got that crazy feedback solo at the end of it—that's just a microphone feeding back and kind of cutting out."

Schmersal admits today that, when he joined Brainiac around 1993/1994, he "was really hungry to be a part of the songwriting."

"I think Tim quickly realized like, 'Oh, it's better not to fight him or whatever about this,'" he laughs.

Then, as always, Brainiac hit the road and toured some more.

In 1994, Brainiac—featuring Schmersal for the first time on lead guitar—played in Lexington, Kentucky, with Rodan, who by then were putting the finishing touches on *Rusty* for Corey Rusk's Quarterstick Records, a Touch and Go imprint. Brainiac also played in Green Bay, Wisconsin, with Jawbox, then at Dayton's Palace Club with Shellac.

They followed Jawbox through Connecticut, Massachusetts, and West Virginia. Then, days before *Bonsai Superstar* was released, they performed with them again at the Blind Pig in Champaign, Illinois.

Schmersal, as a child, admits he aspired to do stand-up comedy. That resonated as he took stages each night throughout the US—and in the van between dates.

"One of the things I realized pretty immediately on tour is it was a great place to try out material and mess around with people," Schmersal jokes. "So, we would record crank calls and stuff. We would just open up the phone book and crank call people."

The band in 1996: l-to-r, Juan Monasterio, Tyler Trent, Tim Taylor, John Schmersal. Photo by Chuck Prezybyl.

Onstage, though, it was all business.

"They were pretty relentless about touring," says Schmoll, the former Pink Lady musician who sometimes sold merch or tinkered with the live sound at Brainiac shows. "They were very serious about what they were doing. 'OK, we're going to make this happen!'"

Brainiac toured again with Girls Against Boys, hitting San Francisco and Boulder, Colorado. They later joined Shudder to Think and Sunny Day Real Estate in Minneapolis, Milwaukee, and Chicago.

With the new lineup, Brainiac played Chicago's Metro in early December. They ended a busy year with a show at the

Black Cat in Washington, DC, on December 16.

Scott McCloud remembers Brainiac supporting Girls Against Boys on the road a while after the latter had released *Venus Luxure No. 1 Baby.*

Tim Taylor chats with Jesus Lizard guitarist Duane Denison while on tour in California. Photo by Michelle Bodine.

"I get my timelines mixed up but, soon after that, we started playing shows with Brainiac as support," McCloud says. "Girls Against Boys was also doing a lot of touring with Touch and Go labelmates the Jesus Lizard, and it wasn't long before all three bands were playing on the road pretty consistently together."

"The point being Girls Against Boys and Brainiac hit it off like a house on fire from the get-go," he jokes. "They were up for touring all the time."

Next up? Another record.

"It wasn't like we were a band that hadn't made a record

in five years," Schmersal says. "But, when you're that young in your career, I think that it felt like it was overdue."

Brainiac trekked back to New York—specifically, Brooklyn—to record its sophomore LP, with Eli Janney again handling engineering and production. (The LP was mixed at New York's Ward Joe, then mastered down at Ardent in Memphis.)

There was more of a degree of experimentation while recording *Bonsai Superstar* than there was on the band's debut, which had been cut with Bodine just a year or so earlier. Schmersal, a creative force on his own, made his mark early, contributing and writing guitar sections for the track "You Wrecked My Hair."

Brainiac also seemed to get a bit of a thrill toying with notions of "found sound" on the new recordings. Shortly before the Brooklyn sessions, Taylor had purchased a weird and somewhat random record—an instructional piece for parrots—in a store in Knoxville, Tennessee. He included some of its voice samples on "Fucking with the Altimiter." To achieve the preferred effect on the song, Taylor sang parts of his vocals in front of a fan, thus the stuttering.

"When we went in to make that record [*Bonsai Superstar*], it was pretty raw and fresh," Schmersal says. "It was pretty spontaneous compared to anything else that we did in the future, that I was involved with. There wasn't any time to meditate on what we were doing. I think that things just kept lining up for us and we were just chasing after the carrot as we went."

"[Brainiac] was basically, exactly, the band that I would want to be in," Schmersal adds. "It really was the perfect band for me to join for what I was doing."

If *Smack Bunny Baby* was a summer record, *Bonsai Superstar* most definitely portended a strange winter. Grass Records released Brainiac's second LP, a thirteen-track affair, in November 1994, right around Thanksgiving.

Right from the get-go, the thing was weirder. Schmersal, the band's newest member, opened the LP with the meandering palm-muted guitars of "Hot Metal Doberman's." Taylor's Moog demanded more attention on the band's second outing, introducing pieces like "You Wrecked My Hair" or providing percussive thrust to the choruses of "Sexual Frustration," one of the finest songs the band ever cut to magnetic tape.

Bonsai Superstar also was nothing if not eclectic. It featured New Wave romps whose guitar parts sounded inspired by surf-rock ("Juicy [On a Cadillac]"), velvet-laced lounge-act satires ("Flypaper"), riotous barn burners ("Radio Apeshot"), even an awesomely quirky sound collage ("Transmissions After Zero"). In the record's second half, the rhythmic "Status: Choke" forced listeners to dance with its infectious, almost ska-informed lead-guitar attack. The record closed with the oddly muted "Collide," the kind of "ballad" a malfunctioning robot with heartache would write, as well as a forebear to the excellent "Silver Iodine," a track the group would compose a year later.

Bonsai Superstar had it all—Brainiac's cup overfloweth, as the fella said. Some thirty years later, the LP still stands as the band's finest, most completely realized work—and most definitely the best surviving document of its overall sound in the studio.

MUSICAL INTERLUDE: "HOT METAL DOBERMAN'S"

*B*rainiac's debut had opened by inundating the listener with distortion and volume. But the band members chiseled their introductions down to the bone to kick off 1994's Bonsai Superstar.

Schmersal, the newest addition to the band, steals the spotlight for the first few measures of the song. He plucks out a 4/4 march with exquisite palm-muted guitar—the repetition occasionally accentuated by Trent's sparse but metered percussion. The opening, despite the rigidity of the palm-muting, really swings and introduces listeners to a state of disorientation. It's hard to tell what gravity is doing, as if the horizon is facing the wrong direction. Taylor adds to the carnivalesque sense of otherness with his highly distorted, even grizzly narration—robot-voiced, but also with a little Moog wiggle in some of the delivery.

The group tosses in some punctuation here—a few twisted notes of rhythm guitar, an incidental vocal aside. But there's a kind of plodding pace to the verses, which makes what's to come later so differentiating, so liberating.

Again, pulling from the Pixies' playbook, Brainiac teeters between the quiet and the loud, messing with the magnetic pull between the two poles. Their homage to Pixies' Black Francis and—more importantly, perhaps—Kim Deal, though, sounds nothing like what Kurt Cobain did on Nirvana's anthemic "Smells Like Teen Spirit." Instead, Brainiac goes from the disturbed to the just-plain-insane, with Taylor switching between his Mr. Roboto–isms and that shrill falsetto he employed so well.

The chorus erupts, Trent really attacking the cymbals on his drum kit.

"Who do you think you are? / Some kind of bonsai superstar?" Taylor whines in falsetto. "Hot metal doberman's, modified with cinnamon fins!"

Though the song's early couplets are all pockmarked with faux-Surrealistic colors and phrases—"a wilted flower girl," "milkshake shivers," "stealing up the hour like a pool cue"— Taylor really gets down to big business later. It's hard not to read a measure of autobiography into the closing lines of the second chorus: the acknowledgment of outsider status, combined with a Jon Spencer–style invitation to throw all that crap out the window and just get down.

"All over town, we were under the ground / Ya gotta whip it up and get up before you get down," whines Taylor, with a second even-higher falsetto occasionally tracking behind him. "I should've never took a chance / But, man, she could dance."

The band walks through this twisted little dance a few times, each pass through with different, peculiar "incidental sounds" from Taylor or guitar accents from Schmersal.

"But, man, she could dance!"

5. "THEY WERE JUST GETTING BIGGER AND BIGGER"

"Silence!

"That's what my girlfriend says, when she's kicking out the teeth of some guy who thinks he's president," Taylor sings on "Hot Metal Doberman's," which opens *Bonsai Superstar*. "A whack cat / That's what my girlfriend says."

That girlfriend was Krista Miller.

For the record, surviving band members noted, Taylor also penned Miller into the lyrics for "Flypaper": "Can you say your dirty words / And balance a book on top of your head? / How silly you look!"

Miller, more recently Krista Putnam, started dating Taylor after the two met at the University of Dayton around 1994. It all started—of course—at a show. She was familiar with Brainiac, having caught the band in its Bodine era when they played at Canal Street Tavern.

"I don't remember what show, but it was in Dayton—and it was kind of ridiculous," Miller told me. "I was looking for a ride home, or I was getting a ride home with friends and [Tim] overheard and said, 'Well, I'm going your way.' So I sent my friends home, and then it turns out that he didn't have a car. He was just going my way. That was pretty cute."

Like others, Miller—who today is a health-care software worker living in Portsmouth, Ohio—came to learn that Taylor was not the same man offstage that he was when performing with Brainiac.

"I think we were both a little quieter, I guess," Miller recalls. "He was definitely more serious. I don't want to say introverted, that's not quite right. But he was very interesting. He was really funny. You know, we laughed a lot, joked a lot. And there wasn't always a huge drive to be around other people. I guess he didn't totally change personalities when it was one-on-one. He was still very intense. But he also was focused."

Miller said their roughly six-month-long romantic relationship "was very intense."

"It was something else," she laughs.

Before entering the circle of friends that included Brainiac band members, Miller went to the Oakwood High School prom with Scott Bodine, the brother of the future Brainiac guitarist.

"They [Brainiac] were really fun, and obviously Tim was very energetic, charismatic, and, you know, handsome, all that," Miller says. "There were so many shows happening all the time! So that was just kind of what everybody did: just went out to shows."

Don't wait for breathless insider takes just yet, Miller says. Taylor never discussed his songwriting process with Miller and only "sometimes" mentioned things regarding Brainiac. They never talked about what any of his lyrics meant, in part because she never had played an instrument or been in a band.

"I wouldn't have been a person for him to bounce ideas off," Miller admits.

Miller moved to Seattle when she was twenty-three, around the time of Taylor's death. She moved back to Ohio years later.

She trekked to McKees Rocks, a Pittsburgh suburb, around 2021 or 2022 to see Schmersal play live with Caribou. And she still has a soft spot for going to shows that feature Dayton's finest.

"I love going to Dayton and catching up. I try to catch a show a couple times a year."

In the midnineties, as Brainiac's influence started to grow, Tim Taylor dragged Dayton musician and self-described former introvert Mike Volk out of his shell. More specifically, he would pull Volk (sometimes literally) away from his apartment, doing nothing but smoking pot.

Jeremy Frederick introduced the two a few years after Volk had graduated from Beavercreek High School in 1990. Not so incidentally, Volk graduated from the suburban Dayton-area high school one year before Frederick. And Schmersal. And Trent.

Taylor and Monasterio went on to become vocal champions of Volk's shoegaze-inspired band Honeyburn, even inviting the group to open for Brainiac in Dayton as one of Honeyburn's first shows. (Taylor learned a lot from My Bloody Valentine, Volk maintains.)

"They took a lot of their own personal time to help me get my musical shit together," Volk recalls recently.

The pair also had given Volk at least three pages filled with "crazy band names" from which they encouraged him to pull a moniker.

He remembers Taylor and Trent coming over to his place

in Dayton after about every time they had toured, playing indie records they had purchased and sharing their war stories from the road.

"Every tour, they were just getting bigger and bigger," Volk remembers. "And their tours started getting longer and longer."

Mostly, though, Volk and Taylor just hung out as friends. When the Brainiac front man was in town, they'd go out drinking or try to talk up young women at parties. When the Dayton bars closed for the night, they'd head over to Woodland Cemetery, one of the oldest rural garden cemeteries in the country, and smoke joints.

"Tim could make a good time out of anything," Volk says. "It's hard to describe, but he was a hell of a mentor. He didn't judge anybody. If you were passionate about what you were doing, he was into it."

Volk also got a glimpse into Taylor's working habits.

Volk—who later formed a band, named Let's Crash, with Frederick—would stay up late writing songs after a night of drinking or partaking in other substances. Taylor, on the other hand, would block out windows of time regularly dedicated to songwriting.

"'Today, from 3:00 to 7:00 p.m., I'm writing songs,'" Taylor would tell Volk. "'I can't go out tonight because I'm writing songs.' He'd just crank 'em out. These things came naturally to him."

Brainiac kicked off 1995 by recording the single "Cookie Don't Sing" at an unknown Ohio location.

The song wouldn't see a release for about two years, when Amphetamine Reptile Records, "AmRep" to those in the know, included the track on its infamous compilation *Dope-Guns-'n-Fucking in the Streets, Volumes 8–11*. Released in April 1997, a month before Taylor's death, Brainiac appeared on the release alongside Jawbox, Servotron, Steel Pole Bath Tub, Boredoms, and more. It took another twenty years for "Cookie" to get her spotlight. In 2021, Touch and Go included the outtake on both of the band's Record Store Day LPs. A schizophrenic, mostly-Taylor-led demo of the song appeared on the priceless *Attic Tapes*; another version of the track lit up *From Dayton, Ohio*.

Brainiac played its first show of '95, a hometown gig, at the club Network on March 11. Another hometown show—with Grass Records labelmates a Ten O'Clock Scholar and the Esoterics—followed at the Lithuanian Club exactly two weeks later.

Then they started to swing for the fences. On March 31 they opened for Unwound at Chicago's famed club Lounge Ax. On April Fools' Day, they played again with Unwound, this time at Chicago Filmmakers.

Some venues became reliable staples with friendly, engaged audiences—such as Sudsy Malone's in Cincinnati, where the band returned to play in June. On other days, they broke new ground. On April 15, they played at Duke University; two days later, they again opened for Unwound—this time in Atlanta.

In the summer of 1995, Brainiac also stormed its largest live stage to date—the second stage on that summer's Lollapalooza Festival. The festival hit stops in Cincinnati and Columbus, Ohio; Tinley Park, Illinois; and Clarkston, Michigan.

BRAINIAC

Flier for show at Cincinnati's Sudsy Malone's Rock 'n Roll Laundry Bar. Courtesy of Michelle Bodine.

Linda Taylor caught Brainiac when the group played on the Lollapalooza stop in Cincinnati. She said her son's demeanor was completely indicative of the multiple masks he was wearing at the time: sensitive and intuitive offstage, and a cross between a deranged carnival barker and a mad scientist catching lightning in a bottle in front of a crowd.

Taylor's mom remembers that show being particularly bombastic, with her son thrashing around and attacking his synthesizers as he belted out Brainiac lyrics.

Tim then left the stage and went back to his mother. Calmly, he turned to her and said, "What'd you think?"

The stage version of "timmytaylor" wasn't a lie, according to people who knew Taylor. But it was most definitely a form of performance.

"[Taylor] is one of the most gracious musicians I've ever

met, always willing to give an interview, pose for a picture, or just talk," one anonymous writer said about Taylor around 1997. "For someone who screams and scowls on stage, he's one of the most polite people I've ever met."

"Onstage, he turned into, completely, this other person," Linda Taylor admits. "It was so much fun seeing him let it all out."

Tim Anderl was part of the crowd that filled local bars, warehouses, university student centers—wherever—to catch Brainiac in its first few years of existence.

Anderl, whose Sweet Cheetah Publicity currently serves as Brainiac's PR machine of choice, first saw the band around the time of his sophomore year at Beavercreek High School. (Yes, the same one from which Trent and others also graduated.) Anderl and his family had moved to Dayton a few years earlier—in 1989, when he was an eighth grader, more specifically—to follow his father's latest officer assignment with the US Air Force. Previously, the family lived in San Bernardino, California.

(Sidenote: Frank Zappa made Tank C in San Bernardino's jail infamous with "San Ber'dino," a piece Zappa and his Mothers of Invention released on their fourteenth LP, 1975's *One Size Fits All*. Zappa lived in a small recording studio in the Inland Empire and performed cocktail music around town. He claimed his ten-day confinement in Tank C stemmed from a bogus pornography investigation the county sheriff's vice squad concocted in 1965.)

The first Brainiac show Anderl caught, he estimates, took place around 1992 at Antioch University in Yellow Springs, Ohio, a village twenty miles northeast of Dayton.

(The original campus shuttered in 2008, amid declining enrollment.)

Brainiac "was huge pretty much as soon as they started releasing their early seven inches," Anderl recounts.

A friend prepped him for Tim Taylor and his eccentricities by making a mixtape that included music from the group's first seven-inch, *Superduperseven*. For a kid and budding music aficionado then listening to bands like Bauhaus and the Cure, Brainiac seemed bizarrely "other."

The show was ferocious.

Brainiac on stage at Chicago's Fireside Bowl in 1996.
Photo by Chuck Prezybyl.

"It was like seeing somebody be electrocuted while playing the weirdest music you've ever heard," Anderl opines. "It was just weird and ferocious and electric. But I've never heard anyone do quite what they did, as well as they did it."

When Anderl was an undergraduate at Ohio University, he caught Brainiac again at Union Bar & Grill in Athens, Ohio.

Earlier, when he was a teenager attending—there's this name again—Beavercreek High School, Anderl also entered Schmersal's orbit.

"I was first aware of John Schmersal because he was active in the drama clubs and stuff," Anderl says. "Actually, the first time I saw John Schmersal—and I teased him about this—was in Beavercreek, a very sort of predominantly upper-middle-class suburb of Dayton. He was in Beavercreek High School's all-white production of *The Wiz*," he laughs. "Oh God!"

Broc Curry started young.

At fourteen, the Bowling Green, Ohio, native got his figurative foot in the door of the "music biz" when he agreed to man the entrance and check IDs at a neighborhood bar known as Club 21. Within fairly little time, he was booking bands to perform live at the venue.

Curry first booked Brainiac to play at Club 21 in early 1994, around the time Schmersal joined the group. He remembers the audience being packed into the bar that night, standing shoulder to shoulder, like so many sardines. The capacity of the place was listed at about forty. Curry estimates two hundred people turned out for the Brainiac show. One or two subsequent Club 21 shows, where a band like Unwound or Trenchmouth played alongside Brainiac, had similar problems with capacity.

"When they played that first show, it was 'Holy crap!'" Curry laughs. "I knew they were amazing from that first show—it was such a high-energy show, it was a blast."

After the success of the Club 21 gig, Curry booked Brainiac in 1995, the year he graduated high school, at

Knownose, a makeshift coffee shop / thrift store next to the police department in Bowling Green. Curry had leased the vacant space for $400 a month. He paid up front for several months because he anticipated a lot of noise complaints and feared the landlord would throw him out right away without money up front.

Knownose's capacity was fifty—at best. When Brainiac played there, between 300 and 350 fans showed up. It was so tight inside that Curry made the entire crowd leave the venue and wait outside in the street each time a band that was playing had to shift their gear between sets.

The evening of the Knownose show ended with a naked man dancing on top of a trash can.

"It was just an insane night," Curry says. "How the cops didn't shut us down, I have no idea."

Between 1994 and 1997, Curry booked Brainiac for about eight or nine, maybe ten, different shows at small Ohio venues that always seemed too small for a band of their caliber. They played a Veterans of Foreign Wars–style lodge in Portage, Ohio, a town of about three hundred people. And a club in Toledo named Whit's End. And Frankie's, a bar and grill that Curry owns to this day.

Curry started hanging out with the group, meeting them after shows at Sudsy Malone's, or elsewhere. After one gig, they all trekked to Corner Grill, a nearby diner open 24-7, to eat grub and swap stories. At the small-town show in Portage, Ohio, the band members talked with Curry about their upcoming record deal with Touch and Go. In Toledo, the friendship was captured on film; Curry appeared alongside the band on the cover of *Muen*, a pre-internet publication lost to the sands of time.

"It was like booking my friends," Curry offers. "Every

time they played, it was packed. And every time they played, they got tighter. And tighter. They were totally unique, ahead of their time—still ahead of their time. There weren't many bands like that.

"I don't know if it was because I was a kid," he adds. "It was such a unique time for music, a time when an indie-rock band meant something."

MUSICAL INTERLUDE:
"GO FREAKS GO"

*I*t starts with a knowing smile and—again—the deployment of that trilling sci-fi B-movie device from the belly of one of Taylor's vintage Moogs.

"Ooh-wah, ooh-wah, ooh-wah," something like an alarm or the sound of a ray gun going off in your pocket.

Pause.

Then, before the band even makes an appearance, Taylor shouts out his call to arms: "Go, freaks, go!"

As the band thrashes out the early refrains of what unfurls to be an MC5-style proto-punk rock anthem, Taylor whips out lyrics—and, more importantly, that delivery!—that are all attitude, his occasional falsetto cracking to reveal spit takes that owe more to the rhythms of urban slang than the foundations of midwestern modesty. (That is, he speeds up and slurs a lot of syllables near the end of a phrase, as a person might turn "with your" into "witcha.")

Again, Taylor's stance as band front man and the kerosene fueling the song's pulsing inertia calls to mind the high-octane Blues Explosion singer Jon Spencer: "Attention check into overtime / Of things that I think about you / One more chance to go yourself / One more shoot for the sprout!"

BRAINIAC

Taylor also builds a lot of tension and heat through the rapid repetition of seemingly irrelevant details. Again, the delivery was key: Taylor worked to make it seem like something sparked in the moment, that he was so caught up in the song that he began extending measures by pounding home a word of phrase. "A trigger, trigger, trigger, trigger, trigger," Taylor stutters at the start of the second verse. "You can't drown, drown, drown, drown, drown / You cannot drown, then what can ya do, what can ya do?" he spits out before a blistering descent into the song's bridge and final chorus.

(Other lyrics seem to fit the musicality or consonance of the words Taylor is using throughout "Go Freaks Go," but not always the intended meanings. A possible example: "I said it's information / That excessive gyration / Throw the thing for a one or a two, yeah!")

What's evident as Brainiac gallops through the verses and choruses is just how tight and refined a working unit they've become. At various times, Taylor and Schmersal sound almost like they're out of sync with Brainiac's rhythm section. We often hear Taylor release the Moog trill that started the song and Schmersal offer guitar figures creeping further up the neck of his guitar as Trent and Monasterio are pounding out a reliable backbeat.

"Bang! I got you / But you can't drown," Taylor barks at one point, his Moog and Schmersal's trebly guitar seemingly in a different meter, a different universe, than the band's bottom end. "You're made outta wood / You can't drown!"

6. "EVERYBODY BELIEVED IN WHAT WE WERE DOING"

Touch and Go Records felt like a family.

The iconic Chicago-based indie label was formed in 1979 in East Lansing, Michigan, as a fanzine by Dave Stimson and Tesco Vee, who later fronted punk-minded pranksters the Meatmen. In 1981, the zine became a proper label when it released a hundred-copy run of its first record, a seven-inch EP by the Necros, who hailed from the Toledo suburb of Maumee.

Corey Rusk, who played bass in the Necros, joined Vee and Stimson at Touch and Go shortly after the EP hit the streets. The trio, tired of the posturing punk embraced by mainstream critics, instead embraced hardcore punk, then in its nascent stages. They became early proponents of the medium, spreading the word—and the music—to hungry listeners in forgotten hamlets across the US.

Touch and Go followed the Necros EP with releases by the Fix, Vee's Meatmen, and Negative Approach. In 1983, Vee handed over full control of the label to Rusk and his wife, Lisa, before leaving Michigan for Washington, DC.

Rusk hired Terry Tolkin, a music-scene insider who later worked for Rough Trade and his own No.6 Records. (And, yes, he was in A&R for Elektra when he signed Stereolab and the Afghan Whigs to major-label deals.) At Touch and Go, Tolkin signed the Butthole Surfers, which became a marquee band for the label. Amid the post-Nirvana "alternative" wave, the Texans made the jump to a major label, Capitol Records, in 1992.

"To me, being on a major label was almost the punchline to a joke," said Butthole Surfers guitarist Paul Leary, in an interview with music writer Ben Graham in the *Quietus* in 2017. "I grew up listening to the Beatles and Grand Funk Railroad and Dean Martin, and the thought of being on the same record label that they were on was too fucking weird, really weird. A lot of people gave us grief for doing that, but fuck: I wasn't going to turn that down."

As the eighties bled into the nineties, Touch and Go evolved into a major player in the underground music scene. Their records sold well, sure, sure, especially for an indie label with a specialized sound. (Rusk later started the Quarterstick Records imprint for work outside his first label's sphere. *Handwriting*, the full-length debut of post-classical chamber act Rachel's, was an early release.)

More importantly, Touch and Go's bands were intensely dedicated to the craft and to hitting the road on tour to share it—and fans responded to that. Though it's likely not the marker by which Rusk measured success, several Touch and Go groups went on to careers on major labels.

Rusk remains intensely private and guarded, even to talk about Touch and Go. He politely declined to be interviewed for this book.

Scott Giampino arrived at Touch and Go around 1992. He started, like most staffers did at the time, in the mail room.

Giampino found an army of like-minded underground aficionados at Touch and Go—among them Naomi Walker, who helped promote tours; office manager Ed Roche; Brendan Murphy, who later succeeded Jim Kimball on drums for the Jesus Lizard; and Howard Greynolds, who went on to manage Iron & Wine and Glen Hansard.

By 1995, Giampino was the label's national publicity director, sending press kits and CDs to a mailing list about five hundred contacts strong, everyone from *Rolling Stone* and *Spin* to local, self-printed fanzines.

"We never had a giant hit," Giampino says. "But everybody believed in what we were doing."

"It really was a family kind of spot," says Greynolds, who started working at Touch and Go shortly after arriving in Chicago around 1993. "Rarely were you gunning for anyone's job. And you liked the people you were working with."

Giampino got a copy of 1994's *Bonsai Superstar* around the time Rusk first developed interest in Brainiac. Rumor has it that Rusk, who many staffers say always had a great ear for talent, was tipped off to Brainiac by Touch and Go artists Girls Against Boys, who had toured with the quartet and were produced by the band's bassist and keyboardist, Eli Janney.

"I had never seen them, but they were weird and fun, and it was rock and roll. You know, it checked all my boxes at the time," offers Giampino, a father of three who moved to Seattle in 2002 and has been booking shows at a venue dubbed the Triple Door for nearly two decades. "Then I saw them. And I was just like, 'These guys are fucking great! This is excellent! I love these guys!'"

Giampino first trekked with Greynolds in a rented car from Chicago to Brainiac's native Ohio to see the group perform live. Neither remembers the date of the show. Or even the venue. But they remember how it made them feel.

"We had a great old time," Giampino says, glowing. "I mean, they were what they were: it was very manic. And rowdy and effusive. They were very energetic, like you were seeing Fugazi."

Years later, Eli Janney says that music writers and fans are still enamored with Brainiac's *Bonsai Superstar* period.

"*Pitchfork* now says it's #57 on their top hundred albums of the nineties, which is hilarious," he laughs. "I'm sure if they came out in the 2000s, they'd be like, 'This is terrible! There's no *Pet Sounds* on it!'"

Giampino started checking out Brainiac every time the group came through Chicago. The band blew up the second stage when the famed Lollapalooza tour stormed the Midwest in 1995. Shows at Lounge Ax and the Empty Bottle were particularly visceral. Greynolds remembers one Lounge Ax show where a crowd member threw a beer bottle "like a rocket" at Taylor's head. He took the hit—and kept playing.

Greynolds also recalls one particularly blistering set at Sudsy Malone's, a Cincinnati landmark that combined loud, underground rock with, um, washing your laundry. A *Spin* writer—yes, *Spin* like a washing machine's spin cycle, no joke—had been in the crowd on the night of that Brainiac show.

"That fucking place," Greynolds quips, "they tore up the place."

"And girls came to those shows," Giampino adds, with a slight chuckle. "And they not only came to the shows, girls danced at those shows."

Greynolds went on to work at labels Thrill Jockey and (briefly) Drag City before founding Overcoat Recordings, which has released music by Richard Buckner, the Frames, and Tortoise with Bonnie "Prince" Billy.

About twenty years ago, Greynolds "discovered" Sam Beam, whose act Iron & Wine he continues to manage. Greynolds also looks after Irish singer-songwriter Glen Hansard, who, with musician Marketa Irglova, won an Academy Award for 2007's Best Original Song for "Falling Slowly" from the indie film *Once*. (Hansard and Irglova have also released music on Overcoat.)

By late 1995, Brainiac had toured extensively, including with "bigger" indie bands like Quicksand and Seaweed.

"Those fans were not really in our scene at all, and their fans weren't really akin to what you'd imagine being a Brainiac fan," Schmersal says. "I think the innocence of it was that they knew we were kind of in that punk, alternative realm. They were like, 'Wow, those guys are interesting.'"

Schmersal remembers that crisscrossing the nation for live shows took some adjustment. Before Brainiac, none of the bands in which he played had trekked for performances beyond Ohio.

"We did five dollars a day, and I think the first day I was on tour we went into a random bookstore, and I bought this book called *Drums*," Schmersal said. "Everyone was making fun of me because I spent, basically, a couple of days' per diem on this book. I didn't have money to eat. So I was just eating from the condiment bar at Arby's or whatever for the first two days. You get sea legs on tour and figure out how to be thrifty and all that kind of stuff."

(Sidenote: While Schmersal joked about Arby's, Trent favored eating at Taco Bell when on the road. On a couple of occasions, pinched for cash, he sometimes would use his five-dollar per diem to buy a box of Frosted Flakes and sustain himself on cereal for a week.)

After the success of Lollapalooza, the band toured Europe. Linda Taylor, Tim's mom, said her son called frequently from the road when on tour.

"I was the worried mom back then," she admits, today a great-grandmother twice over who still lives near Dayton with Laurie Taylor, Tim's sister. "People didn't have cell phones, [and] I remember one time they were in Amsterdam. [Tim] was in a phone booth outside and all of a sudden, we heard what sounded like gunshots. And I said, 'What was that?' 'Oh, just some noise,' he said. And then we heard them again. 'I think that's gunshots,' he said. 'I'm gonna go back in the club.'"

"So," she laughs, "I was glad to see him come home from the road."

Others who had followed the band since its early days, like Taylor's friend Mike Volk from the Dayton band Honeyburn, saw the group's growth during tours as meteoric.

"When they started to take off," Volk observes, "it was

'Holy smokes, here they go!'"

Monasterio, though, tried to keep the interest in Brainiac in perspective. In 1994, a zine editor asked him what the future had in store for him.

"Watch our hairlines recede, our futures get farther away from us—and watch us go on welfare," Monasterio quipped.

Sometime before the first *Hissing Prigs* sessions with Eli Janney, Brainiac hunkered down in Chicago to record in Steve Albini's basement. The buzz on the band was growing. The intention for the session: providing Bruce Pavitt and Jonathan Poneman at Sub Pop Records with material for a Singles Club release.

In the studio, Brainiac continued to burst at the seams.

Trent's drum sound check for the bombastic "Nothing Ever Changes," which was used in the final mix, bore all the charm of Albini's trademark drum sound.

The single never saw the light of day. (Some close to the band say Pavitt and Poneman got cold feet once Rusk got close to a handshake deal with the group.) "Nothing Ever Changes" was deployed as the penultimate track on *Hissing Prigs in Static Couture*. The single "Go!"—a vibrant cover of a Pere Ubu song—later appeared on a Jabberjaw benefit compilation.

(Sidenote: When Brainiac visited the Sub Pop offices in Seattle, they swiped one of the staff member's Rolodexes. Trent fondly remembers prank-calling actor Robert De Niro—he had no idea why the Seattle label had his number—and Courtney Love, Hole front woman and also Mrs. Kurt Cobain.)

Today, Trent says Albini is his "favorite drum producer

on earth." He remembers how oddly outsized the whole experience of working with the Big Black and Shellac mastermind seemed at the time.

"The first thing I saw when I walked into Steve's house was his platinum Geffen Records *In Utero* thing; it might have been gold," Trent offers in a comic deadpan. "And it was just lying against a wall."

MUSICAL INTERLUDE: "VINCENT COME ON DOWN"

As openings go, the one that kicks "Vincent Come on Down" into vicious motion sounds pretty damn urgent.

Trent and Monasterio, a finely oiled rhythm-section machine, pound and pummel and drive forward the descent. Over time-counting snaps of the snare, Monasterio blurts out a Jesus Lizard–esque bass scale that catapults the listener into Taylor's first scream.

On the very next measure, Schmersal announces himself with screechy, detuned guitar chords—single strokes pounded down, down on both the first and second measures—and Taylor's deranged Moog, more Haunted House–inspired than ever. (As the noise-rock anthem unfolds, it becomes incredibly evident these guys have been spending time with Girls Against Boys and the Jesus Lizard. In hindsight, this is their "most Touch and Go song.")

No beat skipped, Taylor, in true rock front man form, starts to snarl and bark out the song's first verse: "Kiss all the babies and rub the politicos / Vincent, come on down!" Now, THIS is a song to light up a crowd. But at what far-fetched version of a party would Taylor and company need to round up the troops so aggressively?

On the choruses, listeners get a bit of a pause—there, again, Brainiac shows what it learned from the Pixies' quiet/loud song dynamics. Trent, though, waxes acrobatic when given free rein to toy with fills, adding a jazzy undercurrent to the piece. Taylor's siren-ish Moogs continue to swirl around Schmersal's decidedly New Wave–colored chords. For a noise-rock or post-hardcore tune, these guys sound practically giddy.

Then there's that lyric. However brief, you can't look past it. By 1997, just a year after "Vincent Come on Down" hit the streets, the closing line of the chorus sounds prescient, even a little bit eerie.

"I don't think you can tell me the things that I want you to," coos Taylor, in falsetto, before stretching the sensually voiced word "cataclysmic" from four syllables to five. "Short of a cataclysmic seduction, nothing can stop my car crash attack on you!"

"Nothing can stop my car crash attack on you"? Ouch.

"Vincent Come on Down," which rides past you like lightning, feels like a much quicker punch to the gut than the song's 2:34 running time first suggests. Even in that short span, Brainiac manages to crank out a bridge that might be its finest—and, without question, most definitely its angriest—to date.

Schmersal's guitar screeches and whines as his fingers climb up the neck of his guitar. Taylor's Moog offers a breathless whirl. "So, come on down," Taylor speak-sings in transition. Then Taylor is joined—punctuated, more accurately—on certain words by the whole band as he shouts out that familiar refrain:

"Two, four, six, eight, tell me who I'm supposed to hate!

I can't quit the goose step; tell me it's a two-step process."

Before launching back into the 4/4 punch of the song's raucous closing measures, Taylor squeaks out a vocal aside that teases the listener: "Da-da-da-da-da-da!" followed by one last fight song–inducing roar, "AHHHHHHH!"

If this thing isn't burned in your memory, you need to listen again.

7. "DON'T MELT ME DOWN TILL THE CRISIS IS OVER"

On October 10, 1995, Touch and Go released its first Brainiac outing, the *Internationale* EP, which had been produced by Daytonian Kim Deal, she of the Pixies and the Breeders. The record featured art identifying some of the world's biggest cities. New York? Yes. London? Check. Tokyo? Absolutely. Oh, and of course, DAYTON.

Four days after *Internationale* hit the streets, Brainiac played Ernst Fall Fest in Ohio. The band returned to the studio to record their Touch and Go full-length debut, and then jumped over the pond, as the saying goes, playing shows in London, Glasgow, Newport, and Brussels.

While in London, in November, they recorded a session for legendary BBC engineer John Peel. (It was broadcast in December.) After returning stateside, they cut another three-song radio session that—again, if you dig deep enough—you can find on the internet.

Brainiac ended its year with a Los Angeles set with Melvins, a show with the Delta 72 at Dayton's Chameleon Club, and another UK date, this time with Mogwai in Edinburgh.

BRAINIAC

●

Touch and Go released *Hissing Prigs in Static Couture*, Brainiac's third LP, and the band's first full-length for the label, in March of 1996. It's also the first recording where Brainiac introduced numbers into their titles and name. From here on out, the group often was stylized as 3RA1N1AC.

The record packed a powerful punch.

The stage-setting or Bizarro-world background noises that propelled *Bonsai Superstar* are missing, replaced by powerful songs towing an oddball line between melody and friction. On "Pussyfootin'," the record's second track, Taylor's falsetto reaches registers that are near cataclysmic, almost comically so. Songs like "Nothing Ever Changes" and "Vincent Come on Down"—Monasterio's punchy bass line bumped up a notch by Trent's urgent smacks of the snare—surged aggressively out of listeners' speakers.

Brainiac, though, didn't abandon its quirkier sensibilities for the over-the-top aggression of a post-hardcore band like Girls Against Boys. A Speak & Spell unit competed with Taylor's faux-whispered narration to great effect on "This Little Piggy." The hazy guitar curtains of "Strung" called to mind the tremendously underrated "Silver Iodine," an understated pop ballad, Brainiac-style, of course, on *Internationale*. "Hot Seat Can't Sit Down" flashed some incredibly pop-informed bridges, and both Monasterio's and Schmersal's parts were dizzyingly full of high-end treble.

Other songs are just plain weird—we're looking at you, "The Vulgar Trade," which centers around a found-sound recording: a man, possibly a South African man, teaches the listener about rocks and metal. The whole LP, though, was wonderfully wrapped up with the anthemic "I Am a Cracked Machine," where Taylor belts out a throat-shredding scream, a few of them actually, over several long measures. At the time, a song like that might have curdled milk. "Bitched up static, burnt cinematic / Tragedy!" Taylor roars. "Don't melt me down till the crisis is over / Not at all!"

"The first lines Timmy Taylor eerily croons on Brainiac's 'Indian Poker (Part 3)' are '*Find my little secret*,' and he might as well be narrating the act of hearing this outlandish, alien music for the first time," Jeff Terich wrote in *Treble Zine* in April 2021.

"A guitar, obscured by a cloud of fuzz, bangs out a filtered, distorted but catchy riff, only to be joined by another in harmony, blaring like air raid sirens as they rise up the neck and toward the eventual verse, in which the tense promise of a thrilling moment becomes a perfect noise rock song," Terich wrote.

"And it's over in 55 seconds."

Touch and Go was no novice on working the machinations of the indie press.

And, sometimes, the label worked the non-indie press. Take, for example, *Sassy* magazine—yes, that *Sassy*—which issued a "Cute Band Alert" for Brainiac around 1996.

"We'll take brilliant minds over pretty faces any day, but it sure is nice when brains and beauty come together in one tidy package," the magazine wrote in a capsule piece. "The Ohio quartet's music . . . is a sonic science project, a genius formula of distorto-cool and hyper-heaviosity, and in terms of looks, well . . . *look!*"

Sassy went on to warn its female readers to not confuse

Monasterio's last name with the popular remedy for yeast infections. More than twenty-five years later, Brainiac posted the piece to its website.

The Internet Archives' Wayback Machine, which works to index the internet back to its earliest days, turns up little in the way of contemporary web-based reviews of *Hissing Prigs*. To be fair, in 1996, most outlets still were predominantly dedicated to their print products.

But the Wayback Machine did churn up one review of the LP from 2004, seventeen years before the *Treble Zine* rave, yet still several years after Taylor's death. A Brainiac fan, writing anonymously on the lost-to-time website Connor Choice, called the LP "amazing, up there with *Doolittle*," one of the Pixies' masterworks.

"It's amazing how something so ugly can sound so beautiful . . . you got to hear it for yourself," the fan wrote. "I cannot stress enough the importance of *Hissing Prigs*. If more kids had been listening to this during the nineties, our American music scene would not be in such a bourgeois state."

"This band is chaotic and deliberate at the same time," a writer who self-identified as the Squealer wrote in 1996, after Hissing Prigs was released. "They churn up a tornado cloud and drop it exactly where it needs to go. Their performance is a shameless salute to the unreasonable side of human nature."

Pitchfork, that cultural gatekeeper, wasn't around to cover *Hissing Prigs* live. Their staff, however, later named the LP the seventy-third best record of the nineties posthumously, in one of those clickbait-driven Top 100 lists.

"Bridging the gap nicely between the nearly quaint spazcore of *Bonsai Superstar* and the outwardly experimental

Electro-Shock for President EP, *Hissing Prigs in Static Couture* boasts three of Brainiac's best compositions: the one-two punch of 'Pussyfootin' and 'Vincent Come On Down,' and the penultimate frenzy 'Nothing Ever Changes,'" *Pitchfork*'s Nick Sylvester wrote on the website.

"Bands don't come much tighter than Brainiac were at this creative zenith, and *Hissing Prigs* finds these Daytonians unusually in control of their rabid freakouts, even maintaining their earlier releases' charming uneasiness," Sylvester wrote. "At all times [Taylor] managed weirdness without alienation, a balance that so few vocalists venture to strike in the first place, let alone achieve with this magnitude."

Scott Giampino hasn't saved the press kit for *Hissing Prigs in Static Couture*, which bore the catalog number TG#155. In the press release accompanying the CD, he remembers throwing around words like "spastic" and "manic" a lot.

The press push paid dividends.

"That record just—I mean, 'exploded' might be the wrong word, but they kind of exploded," Giampino laughs. "They were all over the place. They were getting name-dropped. They were getting some great press and good radio. And their tour was getting great coverage."

(Sidenote: Before Taylor died in the spring of '97, he dropped a couple of hints in the music press about juicy little outtakes from the band's *Hissing Prigs* sessions with Eli Janney. One of the songs the group never released—at least to date—was titled "Sugar Coma." Taylor told one reporter he liked that piece more than some songs that appeared on the LP.)

Jason Pettigrew, the Pennsylvania-bred music writer and *Alternative Press* editor, remembers catching Brainiac live around the time Touch and Go released *Hissing Prigs*.

He joined a crowd two hundred fans strong at the Grog Shop, a Cleveland club about six miles east of the city's skyscraper-defined downtown. The Tucson-based lo-fi duo Doo Rag opened—"an even more reductive Blues Explosion," Pettigrew jokes. (In time, Doo Rag would go on to support both Sonic Youth and Beck at live shows.)

Pettigrew remembers Brainiac lighting up the crowd, minus two or three hecklers "dressed like rockabilly Bettys," he says. ("She's such a mean little girl," Schmersal shot back from the stage.) Taylor was already a pro at handling dissent in the crowd; the entire band surfed right past and put on one hell of a show.

"If you like music held together by centrifugal force and nothing else, Brainiac is on your radar," Pettigrew maintains.

The music writer also stresses that it was Brainiac, before many others, who carved a path for the electronic acts that followed. Some critics suggest nineties-era LPs that broke ground in the electronic space—one cited Beck's *Mutations*, which DGC Records released in November 1998—would have been impossible without Brainiac setting the stage.

Did Radiohead's Thom Yorke listen to *Bonsai Superstar* before writing the faux-machine parts and phaser-gun accents of "Paranoid Android," off its 1997 masterclass *OK Computer*? Did *Electro-Shock for President* portend *Kid A*?

"In the indie-rock scene, everything was guitars, guitars, guitars," Pettigrew says dismissively. "Brainiac brought in electronics and just turned everything upside down in a great fucking way.

"It seemed like they could do anything," he adds.

"Nothing was contrived."

MUSICAL INTERLUDE: "70 KG MAN"

That guitar line.
As with any Brainiac song, the band's two guitars are treated with and filtered through all sorts of experimental touches and recording-studio colors. Schmersal's main guitar line on "70 kg Man," though, might take the prize as one of the group's strangest.

Schmersal opens the song alone, strumming his Teisco Del Ray aggressively, almost blurring the nuances between the notes. And the sound is totally alien: an oddball combination of melodic white noise or a distorted guitar filtered through a crappy tube amp with a cord whose frays are disrupting the signal. This isn't the first time Brainiac tried to capture what might be the sound of a possessed shortwave radio—but it is the best.

The song also flashes other then-trademark elements of the band, such as Schmersal driving forward with the repeating guitar refrain as the rest of the band jumps in with quick punches of sound on certain measures. In "70 kg Man," the device, when combined with Schmersal's desperate-cry-for-help guitar, heightens the tension.

Taylor's voice adds to the punch and pull. On the verses,

Taylor toys with a bass-heavy, businessman-esque narration whose matter-of-factness is at odds with the cacophony that surrounds him.

"Mistakes, mistakes, we are owed," he intones, the word "owed" stretched for a couple extra syllables. "Reason restate manipulate and do it again."

As a rock lyricist, especially from a more technical or writerly perspective, Taylor is in fine form here. He drops in and bends his voice to enunciate great internal rhymes: "Wake the tragics, then shine out the magnets, then fire up the hissing machine" is a classic example.

He also flashes incredible turns of phrase: "Humanoid blueprint nicknamed catch of the day." He even drops biblical references, such as one to Lot's wife that just rolls off his tongue: "the hero steps off in the pillar of salts."

Taylor deploys very mature vocal melodies on the song's bridge, whining out quick blurts of phrases as Schmersal's fingers slide up and down his guitar's neck: "Get the guards / Run them over / Cracker smash the gate."

And, of course, Taylor nails the chorus. All the guitars drop off and we're left with a roiling rhythm section and Taylor's businessman narration, here complemented by a second Taylor backing track: "Three cheers, one kiss, and a punch / We love him like a shot of crutch / So let's all give a warm, warm hand / To the 70 kilogram man!"

The song pulls itself apart by the seams in its closing bars, with Trent letting out a great little yell as he slams the cymbals in faux frustration.

Taylor repeats the word "mistakes" at least eight times, a kind of concluding observation.

8. "ELECTRONIC. AND SO AGGRESSIVE."

Brainiac knew what it was doing as it shifted toward more of an electronic sound.

The band members, according to interviews from the time, made the conscious decision to pursue a new direction. So, on Taylor's cue, Schmersal bought a new digital synthesizer, Trent some drum pads for electronic triggers, and Monasterio a KORG device that would morph his four strings into a synth.

"After we did *Hissing Prigs*, we figured we'd done enough records with the same basic sound," said Taylor, in an interview circa 1997. "All the new equipment brought about a different way of working as a group. Making music is exciting for us again. I think the *Electro-Shock* EP is a bit more pop-oriented than some of the stuff we've done in the past. The most noticeable difference is that the songs have a stronger melodic sense."

"I wouldn't call it punk rock—it's definitely not music to beat people up by."

The world at large first heard Brainiac's new sound on April

Fools' Day 1997, when Touch and Go officially put out *Electro-Shock for President*, its 174th release, on twelve-inch vinyl and compact disc. (Its second edition hits streets in 2019.)

The EP ran just fourteen minutes, top to bottom. Listening in one sitting, though, offered a kind of unified narrative—dare we say, a song cycle. The bits of color or texture in one of the EP's six songs seemed to have symbiotic relationships with measures or a hook in another. The music wasn't composed as much as it was curated.

In case listeners couldn't tell that *Electro-Shock* departed from the band's previous path, the man behind the sound (somewhat literally) of their first three LPs—Eli Janney—was missing. Instead, the band recorded much of the material on its own and pasted or mixed everything together with avant-leading producer Jim O'Rourke, then in the midst of his career with Chicago-based critical darlings Gastr del Sol. The group playfully refers to it in the liner notes as "boogie switching." (In a few years, O'Rourke, as a producer, would go on to construct Wilco's ambitious sound on *Yankee Hotel Foxtrot*, arguably the first great LP of the twenty-first century.)

Taylor made *Electro-Shock for President* different in other ways as well—no matter how small. For the first time on a Brainiac record, for example, fans now could read Taylor's lyrics.

"I'm sorta rebelling against the previous records, just because I felt like on our old records, like, not only were the lyrics not available but they were completely un-understandable, y'know, illegible," said Taylor in a spring 1997 interview with a website whose name since has disappeared from the internet.

"I just tried to make the lyrics clearer this time and print them," he added. "I figured, like, I agonize over those lyrics for weeks and weeks when I'm writing them, so I might as well at least let people know what's going on."

Daytonian Kelley Deal, Kim's twin sister and guitarist for the Breeders, said Brainiac had remained "liberal with song structure" on the new EP, as they departed from working on some of their old turf.

"They still made radio-friendly music," Deal told music writer Leo DeLuca in 2023. "Only they made it electronic. And so aggressive."

Critical response to the EP that has survived the last twenty-five years sounded overwhelmingly positive.

"*Electro-Shock for President* is more of a naughty teaser than an actual follow-up to the acclaimed full-length *Hissing Prigs in Static Couture*, but Brainiac uses every second to its fullest, giving a tantalizing glimpse of the sonic trickery and audio mayhem of which it's capable," *CMJ* magazine wrote in 1997.

"While Brainiac is primarily a rock unit that keeps its electronic leanings in the background on most of its recordings, *Electro-Shock* . . . brings the bleeps and bloops front and center, resulting in a warped, nearly frightening interpretation of rock n' roll as played by an android on the brink of a meltdown," the magazine's unnamed author wrote. "Brainiac fought the machine, and it's hard to tell who won."

Juan Monasterio grew into a band manager indicative of his time.

During the Touch and Go years, and especially in the

band's final months, Monasterio mastered the art of working the phones aggressively to draw just the right people to live shows, the surviving band members remember. As a manager, the band's bassist had terrific organizing skills. He also handled the band's art design, specifically its album covers.

"I was definitely the least technically proficient musically—by far," Monasterio laughs. "But I definitely did all the art. I did all those. I was the band's manager, and [dealt with] all of that stuff: making the T-shirts, booking the shows, talking to the record labels. All of that stuff went through me."

But what Monasterio really had was talent with pre-cell-phone-era networking, Schmersal says. He knew how to work the landlines. (For frame of reference, Brainiac predated the iPhone by a good decade. The band played its last live shows in May 1997. Apple's first "smart phone" was released stateside on June 29, 2007.)

"[Juan] was just calling, then calling other people based on those people that he called," details Schmersal. "It really blows my mind to think about it. I just really don't know how he ended up connecting all those dots and making the extra stuff happen, because any band that's worth their salt has a creative person in the band. But, you know, nine times out of ten, that creative person isn't necessarily the business person in the band. And, you know, Juan and Tim were just a really great pair."

Scott Giampino, from Touch and Go, also got a behind-the-scenes glimpse of Brainiac life too.

Cash Money, the band in which he kept time as the

drummer, played a number of shows with Brainiac and the Delta 72, another Touch and Go act.

Cash Money played its final shows with Brainiac in the spring of 1997, a three-show, three-night run between April 18 and 20. The last set took place at the Grog Shop in Cleveland.

"Let it just be said that if given the chance to see these bands, go!" an unidentified fan wrote online in a review of a Brainiac / the Delta 72 / Cash Money show in Grand Rapids, Michigan, on April 19, 1997.

Brainiac opened that night with "Hot Metal Doberman's" and segued right into "To the Baby-Counter." The live take on "Fresh New Eyes" as well as familiar staples "Vincent Come on Down" and "Sexual Frustration" wowed the crowd.

"[Brainiac] ended with 'I Am A Cracked Machine,' but after Juan and Timmy left the stage, Tyler kept drumming for about a minute while John started rapping," the reviewer wrote. "It was very odd, yet highly interesting. When John was done rapping, he left the stage and Tyler followed with cymbal in hand. It was a classic moment that made up for the shortness of their show."

As the buzz around the band grew, so did the details about its cultural life.

Tyler Trent remembered Brainiac shows as being particularly worthy of name-dropping in Los Angeles. They had been at least numerous times: first at Jabberjaw in April 1994 and again, same venue, in December 1995 with Melvins. Then they hit Pedro's on September 25, 1996.

But the April Fools' Day show in 1997 at Spaceland

in L.A., a kind of faux-release-party for *Electro-Shock for President*, was a trip, connotations intended. Counterculture and sixties drug icon Timothy Leary was backstage, for one.

Afterward, the band went to its first "L.A. party," this one hosted by Sofia Coppola. At that time, the aspiring artist was not yet the acclaimed director of *Lost in Translation* or *The Virgin Suicides*, as much as she was Francis Ford Coppola's daughter. As Trent entered one heavily populated room, he remembered seeing actor Stephen Dorff, who went on to portray "lost Beatle" Stuart Sutcliffe in the film *Backbeat*, mingling with R.E.M. singer Michael Stipe. Wild stuff.

And, Trent remembers, the bouncer wouldn't let in Scott McCloud or Eli Janney or any of the guys from Girls Against Boys.

Broc Curry, the Ohioan who booked Brainiac shows in Ohio, remembers the shift in late 1996 and early 1997. The band's sound was evolving, yes, but so was the general public's reception to it.

Two or three months before Taylor died, Brainiac had played a live set that Curry booked. At an after-party, Taylor gestured to meet Curry in the bathroom. Once there, they hashed out the financial specifics of the show—Curry thinks he paid Taylor about $500 for that night's performance. Taylor talked to Curry about Brainiac flirting with major labels. Taylor confessed he felt he was teetering on the cusp of something.

"It was a great feeling," Curry remembers. "It seemed like things were going so well for them. They were on the verge of something great."

Something great, though, wasn't just necessarily a big-label deal that would've scored some cash—and notoriety—for Brainiac, its surviving band members stress.

"I kind of hate the whole thing about us being signed to a major because we did not sign," Schmersal maintains. "And I think Tim wanted to take things to a bigger level. I don't think the signing part was the big deal to him. I think that just getting the music to a bigger audience was the interesting and exciting part to him.

"Staying true to the music that we were making," he adds, "that was the most important thing."

Electro-Shock for President had barely gone to the vinyl plant for pressing before Brainiac started chipping away at a new LP. Taylor quickly had written three guitar-driven songs he claimed, at the time, sounded almost poppy—more melodic than both *Bonsai Superstar* or *Hissing Prigs in Static Couture*.

The band and, in particular, Taylor continued to question whether Brainiac should follow the electronic-laden path set by *Electro-Shock*—or stick with songs that primarily were guitar-driven. In the spring of 1997, after the EP had come out, he seemed to have made up his mind. Or at least decided on a path and then continued grappling with his choice off the record.

The concept or the sound of the band's fourth LP, however, was at odds with the darkness-tinged electronics of its current release.

"I think [*Electro-Shock for President*] was definitely the most electronic," said Taylor in an interview shortly before his death. "I don't think our next record is going to be this electronic because we've already written some songs that are almost like a reaction against it.

"But the way we're recording 'em, we're demoing them in our studio now, and the way we've been doing it is sort of bizarre—it's turning out electronic," he added. "We're recording a lot of the stuff directly into our computer . . . So, I don't know how it's going to turn out—we're just kind of getting started on it."

Taylor did make one point very clear, though.

"I'm pro both analog and digital, just for the record," he said.

Debby L. Hambrick first caught Brainiac around 1995. Like many, the Washington-bred music lover, who later courted Brainiac as an A&R staffer at Interscope Records, doesn't remember the name of the club the band blew up.

She remembers the sensation, though, of experiencing Brainiac live.

"From the moment Brainiac took the stage . . . everything else in the world melted away," Hambrick says. "Being at a Brainiac show was like tunnel vision, reckless abandon, the fervor of being hit by lightning.

"From the first time Tim took that microphone and howled, I was mesmerized, fixated, obsessed," she adds. "I came to life at my first Brainiac show. Nothing else mattered."

Hambrick called from the first show—it's unclear what landline she used—and left an answering-machine message for Tom Whalley, the former Warner Bros. Records head who signed Tupac Shakur to Interscope back in '89.

"They are the greatest band of all time," Hambrick remembers saying on the machine. "And it is their time NOW."

By 1996, Whalley also had caught Brainiac at an L.A. gig. He told Hambrick to do what she needed to do to get the band to sign with Interscope.

"Use the company charge card on anything you need to till it's done," she remembers him saying.

Hambrick set up shop in "the presidential suite" at the Crowne Plaza hotel in Dayton. But she doesn't remember going over the formal details of a major-label deal with the band.

"It was more like 'I'm with the band and I'm going to make their dreams come true,'" Hambrick says.

The band was flirting with offers at the time from both Interscope and Elektra, the surviving members say. Nobody seems to remember the specifics of the pending deals.

Hambrick felt she understood Brainiac—and, especially, Dayton. She grew up in a twelve-by-sixty-foot single-wide trailer in a small town in Washington: Wenatchee, "the Apple Capital of the World." Her mother, who was raising Hambrick on her own, started embracing Mormonism when Hambrick was twelve in order to give them both some structure.

From a young age, Hambrick wanted out.

After finding punk rock in college, she took a sales position at Colgate Palmolive in Seattle. Though the job didn't speak to Hambrick's passion for music, it did pay well and came with a company car. Shortly thereafter, she made the jump to a more mission-appropriate position at Sub Pop as the Pacific Northwest's music scene was exploding in the early nineties. She remembers picking up snail mail for Nirvana.

After that wave crested, Hambrick moved to New York City and became a publicist, then trekked to Los Angeles to wedge her foot in the major-label door: a receptionist job for Death Row Records. There, rumor has it, she recorded a song with Tupac Shakur, hung out with Snoop Dogg, and handled the office's incoming calls from jail. Soon, she was promoted to an East Coast A&R position—again, back to New York City—under Whalley, then Interscope's president.

Brainiac quickly grabbed her attention.

Hambrick kept super busy. She'd check out four or five bands playing live each night, chat up record store staff, listen to friends' bands or rummage through hundreds of CDs, press packets, and incoming submissions. Former Blondie bass player Nigel Harrison, an Interscope A&R representative, led the way—at least officially.

"Time moved so fast, it stood still during the run-up to them signing their record deal, a fast-paced haze of shows, dinners, hotels, parties, Marilyn Manson at the house in Ohio, Björk being a total bitch in England," Hambrick recalls in a flash of details. "Crowds getting bigger . . . The world was starting to get it. It was all building to a signing day."

Then literally: the crash.

As Hambrick tells it, Brainiac was scheduled to fly to New York after Memorial Day weekend in 1997. The plan was to meet with their attorney to choose between competing deals from Interscope and Elektra and sign a deal memo.

"Everything was so bright, and it was all just beginning," Hambrick says. "It was the start of more dreams. Of creating, celebrating. Instead, the phone rang. I could not process the strange, unimaginable, unfathomable words I was hearing . . . Tim was dead."

"[I thought to myself] 'It didn't happen, I'll wake up,'" she remembers thinking. "It couldn't be. An accident takes him away? He was bigger than that. He would live forever. All of us, we were just beginning to live out our lives, our goals, our visions."

Instead of celebrating at a signing-bonus party in New York City, Hambrick attended a funeral in Ohio.

Hambrick stayed in Dayton for a while; she can't estimate exactly how long. She stayed in touch with Brainiac's band members but, in 1999, there was a merger at Interscope and she was let go. She went back to publicity.

Today, in a twist of irony, Hambrick lives back in Wenatchee, Washington—now with her husband Bill, a physical therapist, and their pets. Her grandson, she declares proudly, is "music-obsessed." Schmersal recently pulled some strings to help get the kid a deal on some acoustic guitars.

During twenty years in the industry, Hambrick says she experienced "so many wild, jaw-dropping, beloved, treasured, feared, and haunted points of life in so many wild and unexpected places on earth."

Brainiac, though, is the story she retells today.

"If you want to know if the story of Brainiac ended in 1997, then you do not know about life and its cycle yet," Hambrick says defiantly. "Just as any other, the Brainiac story has chapters—and they live on. There are Brainiac stories that have not even been written yet. Because Tim's memory and art live on . . . in John, Tyler, and Juan."

MUSICAL INTERLUDE: "FRESH NEW EYES"

"*Flash Ram,*" *the longest song on* Electro-Shock for President, *is the only track on the EP to break the three-minute mark. ("Mr. Fingers," the record's "single" if there was one, comes in one second shy.) But Brainiac set the tone for its new EP—and the electronic sound it had been developing—from the very first second of the very first song, "Fresh New Eyes."*

A sequencer blips out the instrumental opening, little pinpoints of digital percussion floating in the air. Like many rock songs, the time signature to "Fresh New Eyes" falls into the usual 4/4, but the stress on certain notes feels like a suggestive hint toward polyrhythmic composition.

This lasts less than twenty seconds. Then Taylor enters, his voice uncharacteristically muted. It evens sounds kind of exhausted.

"There's a plastic man in a sports car," he mumbles. "And he knows that he knows it all / His plastic features are smiling / as he scrapes them against a wall."

A menacing synth wash appears—a little deeper, more resonant than the percussive bleeps driving forward the piece.

"There's a cover girl on a stakeout / As a worm on a hook, she's bait," sings Taylor, a knotted little guitar line from Schmersal

building in the background, kind of bubbling.

Then the falsetto and a full bravura shout as the music stays controlled, muted.

"In the trunk of a Plymouth in Memphis / She thinks she's made a mistake!"

Here, Brainiac typically would erupt. Not now, not in 1997. Taylor howls out the chorus and there doesn't appear to be a single guitar in sight. The electronic swirl around him largely is unphased.

"Go on and give me some fresh new eyes," he moans, as a synth whirs out a single, trebly note. "Dress my tongue in a new disguise / Go on and give me a sexy mouth to taste it."

Performances of the song sounded dramatically different from the studio recording. When Brainiac played this live, Trent would explode on the chorus, pounding the snare for time and assaulting the ride and crash cymbals.

The surviving document, though, paints a much different picture. In this version of Brainiac's narrative, Taylor is the one struggling to contain his emotions—doing the familiar and playing for the crowd, maybe. The electronics, in turn, offer a firm foundation, a scientific control, a series of sounds unaffected by the band's charismatic singer.

"Go on and give me a sexy mouth to taste it," he blares. "To taste it!"

9. "I WANT THIS TO MEAN SOMETHING"

"Dead, dead, dead, dead, dead—he's fucking dead!"

Singer-songwriter Jeff Buckley, sporting a gray dress suit and tie, paused his May 26, 1997, set to lament about Tim Taylor's death and the assumed demise of Brainiac in front of a crowd of fifty or sixty people at Barristers' Bar in Memphis, Tennessee.

Taylor had died just three days earlier.

Buckley, the estranged son of seventies folk icon Tim Buckley, then segued into his now-famous cover of Leonard Cohen's "Hallelujah," which he dedicated to Taylor.

"The guy from Brainiac is fucking dead!" Buckley had spat out. "I want this to mean something to every fucking one of you."

Buckley closed his short set that night with what one fan called an "aggressive" cover of Edgar Winter's "Frankenstein." Sadly—and ironically—the show where Buckley paid homage to an ascending musician killed too soon also was his last.

Buckley, a Gen X icon who struggled with the fame he achieved throughout his young life, drowned three days later in the Mississippi River.

Buckley was thirty years old.

Garin Pirnia grew up in Dayton, graduated from high school in 1995, but she never got to see Brainiac play live.

In 2018, Red Lightning Books published her musical trip through the Buckeye State, *Rebels and Underdogs: The Story of Ohio Rock and Roll*. In it, she profiled Brainiac, among many others. "James Brown meets Devo on acid" was how she first described the group, fittingly.

"Knowing more about it now, after Tim died it just ended the whole Dayton music scene," says Pirnia, today a freelance writer in Covington, Kentucky. "There's a sense of community, and that music? You won't be able to replicate that.

"I don't think a lot of people even knew there was a scene in Dayton," she offers. "And it'll never happen again."

Tyler Trent remembers the day of Taylor's death well.

It was late Friday morning, and he woke up to the sound of someone leaving a message on his answering machine. It was Dave Dobin, Tim's roommate. Trent called him back and quickly sensed something was wrong.

"Just come to the house," Dobin kept saying.

"Instantly, I put it together," Trent remembers now. "Something had happened to Tim."

Around noon, Trent drove to Taylor's house near Main Street, about twenty-five minutes away from where he was staying at the time. When he got to the house, Taylor wasn't there.

Trent still remembers Dobin putting his hand on his

shoulder and saying, "Tim's dead."

"I was completely emotionless," Trent recalls. "I just didn't know how to react."

Dobin offered Trent one of the band's signature drinks, a "John Glenn," essentially just vodka and Tang. Trent passed. He hugged Dobin and left.

Trent drove back down Main Street. As he neared a BP gas station, he saw the metal utility pole Taylor had hit the night before. It was bent over almost ninety degrees and charred by the flames.

"I pulled into that BP and I just lost it," Trent remembers. "I called my dad first, I don't know why. And I started scream-crying that Tim was dead."

Taylor's death, though, wasn't the end of the Brainiac story.

At first, the remaining band members splintered.

Trent once was credited as Claire Quilty, a reference to a Vladimir Nabokov protagonist and sexual deviant, on Brainiac's sophomore LP. He used his own name, however briefly, when he played drums in the Breeders. He moved with Jeremy Frederick, "the fifth Brainiac," and Taylor's old friend Mike Volk to New York City as the Breeders worked on an LP that 4AD never would release. Their time in North America's biggest city bottomed out, as the failed sessions for the record the band later would go on to rerecord and call *Title TK*.

Trent, Frederick, and Volk would move into a studio apartment somewhere in the city, get kicked out, then move into another. The amount of illicit substances abused during this period is disputed.

This lasted just a few months.

To hear longtime Brainiac fan Griffin Hamill say it, drummer Jim Macpherson, who played with the Breeders from 1992 to 1997, didn't stand a chance against a live wire like Trent.

"Jim plays a song, but Tyler hits a song," Hamill observes. "It's interesting, too, because he's such a sweet guy."

Kim Deal first had asked Trent to play a memorial show for Taylor that her then-buzz-worthy group headlined at a Dayton club. Then came the New York adventure. Shortly after that, Trent's mounting drug problems started to obscure, to get in the way of, his work. He left the Breeders and didn't play the drums for several years.

Until 2002.

After a period without any musical output, Trent joined Frederick, his former Sunken Girraffe bandmate, in a trio based in Dayton called the Dirty Walk. But it never really took off.

Monasterio's post-Brainiac years, musically speaking at least, were even thinner.

The band's most reserved member directed a video in 2003, then formed and briefly played in the post-whatever band Model/Actress alongside former Scratch Acid drummer Rey Washam. That group released one record, a self-titled EP, through Chicago-based label Thick Records in 2006.

Schmersal's working life in music rebounded the quickest of the surviving members. It also has displayed the longest shelf life.

"I know you have music in you," Howard Greynolds, the

former Touch and Go staffer, said he wrote to Schmersal in a letter sent after Taylor's death. "Don't let it end."

In 1998, the year after Taylor died, Greynolds released Schmersal's first post-Brainiac music, a seven-inch on All City Crossroads under the project name Enon. Schmersal recorded its A-side, "Fly South," in Brooklyn. The B-side, "The List of Short Demands," was cut at a Masonic temple in Newport, Kentucky, just an hour's drive from Brainiac's Dayton.

A year later, See Thru Broadcasting released a full-length, thirteen-track solo debut from Schmersal under the name John Stuart Mill, who was a real-life British philosopher and political economist.

Enon press shot: l-to-r, John Schmersal, Matt Schultz, Toko Yasuda.

The Enon story could be another book. Schmersal later expanded the 1998 side project into a full-fledged band with Rick Lee and Steve Calhoon—two alumnae of Skeleton Key, a quirky indie group with whom Brainiac had played shows. For most of its twelve-year run, however, Lee and Calhoon weren't in the picture. Schmersal instead wrote, recorded, and toured alongside Toko Yasuda and Matt Schulz.

Schulz, perhaps not so incidentally, is Trent's cousin.

In the years that followed Enon, Schmersal formed two more bands—Crooks on Tape and Vertical Scratchers. He also toured for the better part of a decade with the group Caribou.

As of 2023's end, the record-cataloging website Discogs lists ninety-five credits—official releases—under Schmersal's name.

Shortly after Taylor's death and before Enon became a fully operating music machine, Schmersal found himself at a dead end: living in Newport, Kentucky, without a car, and working a job making burritos at a bar in Cincinnati.

So he fled for New York City. Once there, he first took a construction job, then worked in a Kim's-style video store, where film aficionados could snatch up obscure titles and cult foreign films in addition to the latest Hollywood fare. (He calls the place "highfalutin.") Around 1999, Schmersal got a gig laying Ethernet cable and went on to help businesses, mostly a lot of law firms, prepare for the Y2K attack.

Y2K, again for the record, never happened.

During the dot-com boom in the early aughts, Schmersal also tried to combine a day job with his music career, writing and recording theme songs for Funny Garbage, a short-lived agency that developed content for places like Cartoon Network and Nickelodeon.

After Taylor's death, Schmersal continued to be identified by his work in indie music.

Though divorced, he keeps in regular touch with his

daughter, who hit age twenty-six in 2023 and is working to become a second-tier wine sommelier in Big Sky, Montana. Schmersal currently lives in California.

Over the years, Brainiac recordings influenced both contemporaries of the Dayton group and those who followed their path.

Cedric Bixler-Zavala and Omar Rodríguez-López made no bones about the fact that Taylor was a huge musical influence on the Mars Volta, and they carried on Brainiac's tendency to embrace quirky sonics into their own recording. The musical pair said they also see Brainiac's fingerprints on bands like Blood Brother, the Locust, and At the Drive-In. No less than Trent Reznor cites the music Brainiac released in its short run as a key influence on Nine Inch Nails.

"I think the lore of Brainiac has just grown so much," says Girls Against Boys member Eli Janney, who recorded Brainiac's three full-length LPs. "They were always an amazing live band. And it's just nice that the interest in that band has really exploded."

"You listen to Brainiac today," says Broc Curry, the Ohio music promoter, "and nobody sounds like Brainiac."

The Brainiac legend continued to metastasize, with some mimicking or paying homage to the group, though nobody ever seemed to be able to replicate their uneasy sound or firecracker stage presence.

The psych-pop outfit Tripping Daisy did some justice to "Indian Poker Parts 2 & 3," from 1996's *Hissing Prigs in Static Couture*. The Dallas-based group recorded and released it as the album closer for their *Jesus Hits Like the Atom Bomb* LP in 1998.

Melvins, Washington-bred Gods of Thunder and childhood friends of Kurt Cobain, gave the lounge-rock satire "Flypaper," from *Bonsai Superstar*, the full-on acoustic treatment—complete with multitracked harmonies—on their *Five Legged Dog* LP, which Ipecac Recordings pushed to streets and streaming services in 2021. (Many prefer Trent's brush-accented drum take to Dale Crover's more straightforward technique.)

Some takes and homages to Dayton's finest were more conventional, more orthodox. Brat Curse, a 2010s-era alt-rock outfit that originated in Columbus, Ohio, gave tribute to their forebears by covering Brainiac's energetic, earworm-driven "Ride," from *Smack Bunny Baby*. The band recorded and released their version as a seven-inch single that Ohio Seven Records cut to wax in October 2016.

Brainiac also has notched multiple homages from contemporaries of the band, many of them nineties-scene staples now on the reunion trail. Man or Astro-man? covered "Nothing Ever Changes" live at the Market Hotel in Brooklyn in 2020. Internet lore claims the Toadies were doing "Flash Ram" live as early as June 1997 at a show in Dallas.

The surviving members of Brainiac, as well as its myriad fans, have started to fan the flames on a legacy that feels outsized considering the band's existence only stretches some five years.

Monasterio, Trent, and Schmersal joined fellow Dayton musician Tim Krug a decade ago to bring the band back to the stage as a tribute to Taylor. The faux–victory lap also introduced the group's music to a new generation wowed by Brainiac's manic cross-pollination of Devo-esque pop structures with the raw DIY energy of the eighties punk underground.

On December 6, 2014, the new quartet first performed as We'll Eat Anything—the name under which Brainiac first formed in 1992—at Blind Bob's, a family-owned tavern on East Fifth Street in Dayton's Oregon District. A standing-room-only crowd turned out for the show, which organizers dubbed "North of Nowhere South," a kind of fundraiser for the recently deceased Brainiac collaborator Jeremy Frederick.

Frederick, a Dayton music-scene staple, had died after storied struggles with substance abuse on August 16, 2012, four months short of his fiftieth birthday. Taylor, who Frederick called his best friend, was named among those who predeceased him in a *Dayton Daily News* obituary.

"The Dayton music community has long had a unique 'band of brothers' landscape as far back as anyone can remember," Art "Dr. J" Jipson and Shelly Hulce wrote in the online mag *Dayton Most Metro* in advance, promoting the event. "Taylor and Frederick were, and still are, twin flames—creating remarkable music in amazing bands that dazzled the Dayton community and beyond. At times, their light was bigger than the room. It's obvious those flames have never dimmed."

Earlier in 2014, Krug remembered talking with Trent and Schmersal while Schmersal was visiting Dayton. Schmersal invited Krug to play some Enon songs with them.

"I said, 'Yeah, then we should ask Juan to come [to

Dayton] and we'll play a Brainiac song," Krug said.

It quickly evolved.

"The whole time, it was like, 'I can't believe this is happening!'" Krug laughs. "'This should not be happening!'"

Schmersal told *Dayton Most Metro* that he had toyed with performing songs at the Frederick tribute show by Sunken Girraffe, the outfit he, Trent, and Frederick formed while attending Beavercreek High School. Their bassist was a no-go.

"From there, it turned into doing a Brainiac thing," Schmersal says. "It has never occurred to any of us to reform the band because it is simply not Brainiac without Tim Taylor.

"This is about celebrating the music of our friends with our friends," he adds, "in the community where it came out from."

Schmersal, joined onstage by original Brainiac lead guitarist Michelle Bodine, took front-man duties. Taylor's musical role—second guitar, keys, Moog—was played by Tim Krug, a self-described "proud art-school dropout" raised in the Dayton suburb of Beavercreek. (Krug graduated from Beavercreek High School, like Trent, Schmersal, and others. He just did it in the spring of 1998, a few years after the Brainiac members did.)

"We didn't want to call it Brainiac," Krug says. "We didn't want people coming from out of a town—it was a weird scene.

"But we did it, we did this thing," he adds. "I didn't think it would happen ever again."

Krug, the newest addition to Brainiac, first saw the Taylor-led lineup perform at Dayton's Chameleon Club around 1995. A friend had handed Krug—then a fan of Nirvana, Nine Inch Nails, and Aphex Twin—a mixtape that included some of the band's songs. He caught another two or three Brainiac shows after that, including their Lollapalooza set in Cincinnati. He still remembers attending one of the group's final Dayton shows at the Ballroom in the spring of 1997.

"They were not your average punk band, the kinds of bands you see a lot," Krug says. "When I saw them, it just seemed like they had a good bit of vaudeville showmanship to them that a lot of bands didn't have.

"I didn't really know at the time that they were getting really big—or bigger," Krug adds.

After all, Krug said, there was no social media to gauge Brainiac's growing followers or get analytics on Tweets sharing links to Bandcamp pages. The group never employed a social media manager—the idea of "social media" didn't even exist in 1997.

"They were just a cool band that I would try to go see when they were in town," he says.

Krug, a member of Oh Condor and Hexadiode, later covered Brainiac with Jeremy Frederick in the band Human Reunion. He met his first Brainiac band member—John Schmersal—in 1999 or 2000 at an Enon show at Dayton's Safari Club. The two became fast friends. Frederick handled the introductions to the rest of the surviving band members.

When the idea of "the secret show" in 2014 at Blind Bob's started to materialize, Krug realized he was going to need to learn Taylor's guitar parts—no easy task.

"It was an instant 'Yes! I'll do it!'" he says. "Then you sit down and you look at the guitar and you say, 'How am I going to do that?!'"

Linda Taylor, Tim's mother, called Krug "just such a good fit" for the new Brainiac lineup. She also strongly defends the band members' decision to reunite and play together again, even without her son.

Some people have pestered her with questions about the band re-forming, which—intentionally or unintentionally—are meant to stir up strife and discontent, she says.

"'Doesn't that bother you?' they ask," Linda says. "'I mean, it's Tim's music!'

"All those guys, I just love them to death, and they lost a lot too, because their careers were just yanked away," she says. "They were right on the verge of bigger things happening. I just want all the success for them that they could possibly get. And it is—it's hard that Tim isn't there. I'm not going to lie. But it's also wonderful to see people reacting to that music after all these years."

The band in 2023: l-to-r, John Schmersal, Tim Krug, Tyler Trent, Juan Monasterio. Photo by Don Thrasher.

Mike Volk, an old friend of Taylor's, has chosen to stay away from the reunion shows. He wants to preserve the integrity of his memories of seeing the original lineup, and of Taylor's central role in Brainiac.

"It's just not the same," says Volk, the Honeyburn band member who left Dayton for Cincinnati after Taylor's death and only returned years later. "I don't blame them for doing it. It's gotta feel good to do it. I'm super supportive of it. But, I don't know, it's too much.

"I'm gonna hold dear to those old memories," he adds.

On December 9, 2017—three years almost to the day after the We'll Eat Anything show—the new Brainiac reunited to play a short surprise set at the Bell House in Brooklyn's Gowanus neighborhood. The goal of the evening was to help raise money to complete a documentary, *Transmissions After Zero*, that Daytonian Eric Mahoney was filming about the band. The Bell House show featured performances by Girls Against Boys and Savak. Another band played too: the Heist, a.k.a. the 8G Band from *Late Night with Seth Meyers*, which Eli Janney leads.

"It can be kind of weird," Tim Krug says. "You just get kind of lost in the thought, 'I'm playing a show with, you know, one of my top-five all-time favorite bands.' It can definitely give you a weird existential fear, almost like a panic. At the same time, I just remember that I'm playing songs that I love with three of my best friends, which is kind of what being in a band is. It's fantastic."

Members of Hole, Les Savy Fav, the Dismemberment Plan, and the Wrens roamed the crowd at the 2017 show. Girls Against Boys marked the special occasion by unfurling their own take on the Bodine-era Brainiac staple "Ride."

"It was crazy to see how many young kids were coming

out to these shows," says Eli Janney, who played that night in Girls Against Boys and the Heist. "It's a whole audience that's tapped into this nineties music that they just weren't thinking was there. People were going crazy.

"I'm glad—they certainly deserve it," Janney adds. "The lore of that band has just grown so much. They were always an amazing live band . . . but the interest in that band has really exploded."

The new Brainiac next played for hometown audiences one week later, on December 16, 2017, at Yellow Cab Tavern, a venue set up in a former taxi-cab building in downtown Dayton.

Yes, yes, Brainiac explodes in the live footage unearthed for *Transmissions After Zero*. But the film also featured sage words from some impressive talking heads, ranging from renowned engineer and Shellac front man Steve Albini to the National's Matt Berninger. ("They were heroes of mine then and still are," said Berninger, who fronted Nancy, a band Brainiac members came to see in a Cincinnati basement in 1996.)

The film was funded, in part, by Trent Reznor, a Pennsylvania native who formed Nine Inch Nails while living in Cleveland, and no less than Luke Skywalker—a.k.a. Mark Hamill, iconic *Star Wars* actor and the father of Brainiac superfan Griffin Hamill.

"I NEED TO SEE THIS!" Mark Hamill tweeted at 2:01 p.m. on April 19, 2017. "Hope you can help this documentary about the amazing band #3RA1N1AC get finished & released!"

The *Transmissions After Zero* documentary premiered

in March 2019 at SXSW, about eighteen months after the fundraiser. The creators of the film quickly hit the touring circuit.

"For some, this documentary will fill the gaps in the story of a band they already love. For others, this may well be an introduction to their new favorite band," wrote Matt Shiverdecker in the *Austin American-Statesman* at the time the documentary premiered. "Even twenty years after their last release, Brainiac sound like they're from the future. This documentary is an excellent primer that should help to secure their place in music history."

A month after its release, on April 20, 2019, Brainiac played a weekend show dedicated to the film's premiere at the Brightside in Dayton. Dayton-bred music writer Garin Pirnia was there.

"They show a lot of passion still, twenty-five, twenty-six years later. I think the touring, reuniting, it's been good for them," Pirnia says. "That night, they were enthusiastic and rocked really hard. It was nice to say I was finally able to see them."

The band then trekked to Los Angeles to play during a film premiere at the Regent, a vintage circa 1914 cinema turned downtown venue. Musician and *Saturday Night Live* alum Fred Armisen joined the band onstage for a rousing take of "Vincent Come on Down."

"Eric doing the doc was cool because I always want to do things that will keep the Tim thing going," Monasterio told *Dayton Daily News*, the band's hometown paper, in February 2023. "I feel like that's the most important thing. Anything we can do that keeps that going is a huge win. And it turned out amazing."

BRAINIAC

Schmersal had collected tons of Brainiac demos, live recordings, and studio outtakes and wanted to put them to use. So, in 2021, the band helped release two Record Store Day LPs by Brainiac, one a live collection, the other a set of demos prominently featuring Taylor.

In 2023, Touch and Go continued to feed a fanbase hungry for lost Brainiac material. It released *The Predator Nominate*, a too-short collection of rough sketches for the fourth Brainiac LP for which the band had entered preproduction at the time of Taylor's death.

In February 2023, not wasting any momentum, Brainiac embarked on its most ambitious, most reunion-affirming move to date: a UK tour with post-rock icons Mogwai. Starting February 9, 2023, in Manchester's Albert Hall, the tour hit ten venues in ten days, ending at Birmingham's O2 Institute.

Brainiac on stage at Detroit's UFO Factory in 2023.
Photo by Brian Rozman.

"I love playing these songs," Tyler Trent told me as he prepared to leave Dayton for the UK tour. "I don't care if it sounds braggy, but anytime we revisit this stuff I'm like, 'These are great songs. I'm so glad I was in this band.' I'm just grateful all over again whenever we do this stuff, which is a really cool thing."

Brainiac immediately came stateside for three more February shows—in Detroit, Dayton, and Cincinnati—and returned to Chicago in June for sets at the Empty Bottle and the Do Division Street Fest.

Brainiac plans to make its presence known again in 2024 with yet more touring, including dates in the American South and Southeast.

"It was really exciting to go on these tours," offers Schmersal, who today lives in the desert north of Palm Springs, California. "At our show in London, there were older people, our old-school fans, and people that flew in from all over Europe to see us. But by and large, the majority of the audience were, like, fucking twenty-year-olds. It was really, really cool to see that, a new generation getting that excited about this music."

Griffin Hamill was a teenager living out in California when the buzz around Brainiac started to swell like an approaching storm after *Hissing Prigs in Static Couture* was released.

Hamill was already riding the alt-rock train, listening to bands like Sonic Youth, Nirvana, and Dinosaur Jr., when his brother, Nate, turned him on to Brainiac. More than twenty-five years later, he still can recall the impression *Hissing Prigs* left on him following a first listen.

"I remember 'Pussyfootin'," he says. "I was apoplectic."

Hamill's brother caught Brainiac twice late in their run, both times in L.A.—at Jabberjaw in '96 and the Roxy in '97. Hamill was "within inches" of seeing the band live in their heyday; he doesn't recall the sequence of events that thwarted the evening.

The Brainiac reunion, in short, has helped Hamill cross an item off his bucket list.

He met Monasterio more than a decade ago at Echo in L.A., while a DJ—was it Calvin Johnson?—spun records nearby. Hamill, son of *Star Wars* actor Mark Hamill, notes the irony of being starstruck at the time by an indie musician from Ohio.

"They're probably more celebrities to me than people from Hollywood," he laughs.

The surviving members became fast friends with Hamill and hung out with him when he attended the 2019 reunion show in Dayton. He also caught them later in Chicago, during their first live performance there since 1997.

"It's just cool to see them enjoying the music again, because they couldn't for so long," Hamill says. "I remember John saying, 'It's really about this moment. It's about bringing people together.'"

Hamill also met Linda, Tim Taylor's mother, at the Dayton show in 2019. He gifted her a portrait that he'd painted of Taylor. The two continue to speak on the phone occasionally.

"It sounds corny, but it gets sentimental," Hamill says. "These are good memories for me, and nobody can take that away."

Hamill again has felt "apoplectic" as Brainiac and Touch and Go dig into their archives and release outtakes and found music. His favorite Brainiac LP, the one he flips on the most, remains *Hissing Prigs in Static Couture*.

But he, like many fans, remains curious about how *The Predator Nominate* would've developed as the group's fourth LP. Would it be another statement? Or another segue?

Though all listeners have are some early demos, Hamill doesn't doubt Taylor would've cooked up something extraordinary.

"I guess he always had an album in the bag—it's crazy, how he was able to do that," Hamill says. "But that's Tim."

In an interview recorded just days before his death, Taylor again dropped hints on the workings behind the band's fourth LP.

The British interviewer had heard a new Brainiac song, "Give Me a Myth," which he said "was maybe the poppiest thing" the group had done to date. Would the new record reflect that shift in tone?

"We did the first record, and then every time you do a record it's a natural tendency to react against it and want to do something in the opposite direction," Taylor remarked. "The first record was not pop, but it was more melodic or pop-oriented. We wanted to move away from that, and I kind of want to move back into that now."

Taylor talked about all the major-label buzz, saying the possible decision to ink a deal "always [has] been like a growth thing. There's a pretty good chance the next one will be on a major," he said.

"We wanted to be big enough to be on a major label but didn't want to do it too soon," Taylor added. "We didn't want to burn ourselves out trying to make a big jump."

When it came to writing the new material, Taylor said

he was craving two things: lots of time touring and a good degree of pressure.

"I kind of need a challenge now. I feel like I've done it this way for five years. This is just my personal theory on how things work, at least for me. If I don't have somebody constantly pushing me, and if I start to feel comfortable in any situation, my mind atrophies.

"I don't like to wear comfortable clothes onstage because if I'm comfortable, I don't push as far as I could," he added. "I feel like I need that challenge now. I think that last record we did [*Electro-Shock*] is one of our best records, and I don't think it would've been nearly as good if we weren't stressed out about what we are going to do as far as the major-label thing. Then you just notice things, especially at these shows. There are so many things you do that you can improve upon.

"When you have two thousand people looking at you every second, you just realize there's a lot of room for improvement."

Scott Bodine doesn't mince words about Brainiac.

He got the sense from day one, when his sister was just joining the band, that there was something special about Brainiac—and about Tim Taylor as the center of its songwriting and performance gravity.

"You knew good things were gonna come from those guys," he recalls. "Tim seemed like a 'community' guy. Tim was our age, and he was our guy. I know it's kind of corny. But Tim would've gone on to do great things.

"He was the Prince, the artist Prince, of Dayton, Ohio."

Bodine was at the 1470 Club in Kettering on the night of Taylor's death. He remembers joking with Taylor at the time about his newly purchased Mercedes-Benz.

"[I said] 'Tim, heard you got a new car?!'" Bodine remembers. "I remember looking in the parking lot and it was 'Wow! That is a piece of shit!'"

Weeks earlier, in the spring of '97, Bodine had caught one of Brainiac's last Dayton shows—possibly their final show—at Aardvark, a makeshift venue in the back of a renovated sub shop.

Even today, with Bodine living and working in Dayton after eight years or so in nearby Columbus, he wonders what could have been.

"If Brainiac were to have continued, they would have been the most important band to come out of Dayton," he says, matter-of-factly. "If you saw them live, you'd know. You'd be like, 'Oh shit! Who ARE these guys?!' They had a universal appeal; they were that good.

"Their momentum," he adds, "it would've put Dayton on the map like no other."

EPILOGUE: "SOMETHING'S GOTTA GIVE"

Tyler Trent sits, waiting, at a table for four in a terminal-style, brick-walled market in Dayton, Ohio.

It's a hot day, unusually hot even by summer standards. The year 2023 is half-spent.

Trent, now more of an adult proper than he was during his Brainiac years, sports black-rimmed glasses and a blue, long-sleeve Sunny Day Real Estate T-shirt. His hair, cropped tight, isn't graying so much as it's flecked with salt and pepper.

Trent tells me he rediscovered his faith more than a decade ago.

In 2007, strung out on crystal meth and—oddly enough—morbidly obese, Trent returned to Lifepointe, the nondenominational church in the Dayton suburb of Kettering that he grew up attending. (Joe Anderl, a member of band the 1984 Draft and the brother of Brainiac's aforementioned publicist, also attends Lifepointe services. He later went on to play with Trent during a worship service at Dayton's Yellow Cab Tavern.)

Trent started volunteering at the church—and took any job he could get, really. He then started working there part-time. By the time the COVID-19 pandemic was in full swing, in 2020, he was ordained as one of the church's full-time pastors.

"After Tim died, my personal stories, my trajectory was just out of control," Trent says. "I was doing plenty of recreational drugs on tour. But when Tim died, I just went full-blown professional and just spiraled out of control. That pretty much continued until our kid [Noah] was born. Then I would just relapse. Finally, my wife was just like, 'All right, something's gotta give.' So, in 2007, I went back to that church I grew up in.

"It was crazy, I was a 350-pound crystal meth addict, if you can figure that out," Trent says. "People that want to wag their finger at the evil rock 'n' roll band or whatever, all the stereotypes, it was kind of the reverse. On the road it was all business and just enjoying the music. It was when we were home that I was just falling apart."

He kicked the drugs and lost all the weight, though he admits the latter was part of "a twelve-year gruesome journey." Noah was a toddler when Trent went sober, around 2007. His son, now in his early twenties, is an earth and environmental sciences major at Wright State.

Michelle Bodine walks in with her new fiancé and her daughter, twenty-four, who has Rett syndrome, a rare genetic disorder that affects the way the brain develops. Bodine's wearing all black—black T-shirt, black skirt, black shoes. Bodine and Trent, once bandmates, now live blocks away from each other in Huber Heights, a Dayton suburb.

They chat for a while, grab lunch, share old war stories from the road.

"Dayton always has had an unusually vibrant music scene," says Trent, between bites of a sandwich. "There was always a show."

Then Trent and Bodine get into their respective vehicles and start driving the backstreets of Dayton. As they drive through sometimes-abandoned, sometimes-revitalized streets, both point out spots where Brainiac practiced ("Springfield Street") or warehouses where they performed. Previous "headliners" in these informal jaunts, which sometimes involved Dayton police or firefighters breaking up a crowd and shutting down a show, ran from Fugazi to Green Day.

We stop at another Brainiac hangout spot, a vacant factory that, in the nineties, the band members simply had dubbed "the Front Street building." Somebody recently has repainted its redbrick walls, accenting them here and there with touches of fresh forest-green paint. Today, the building houses other kinds of Dayton artists. A banner hangs on the factory's "annex" advertising Silica Dreams LLC, a self-described creative art studio. In another nook, a craftsman: Custom Wood Creations.

Maybe Taylor was wrong. Maybe some things do change.

Trent jokes about how Brainiac sometimes would be billed at places near Front Street with a common spelling error on the flyer. "Braniac," he laughs. "The high-fiber super-villain!"

Turning his compact car around a corner, Trent points out a house as he drives into the western half of Dayton. Everything is an insinuation about what the house means to him.

"I was a recreational drug user, but when Tim died, I spiraled," he says, plainly. "On any given day, though, I'd rather have bought meth on the east side than crack on the west side."

Trent switches the topic of conversation, talking about how Monasterio was at home one day when he envisioned the cover for *Smack Bunny Baby*.

"He literally just grabbed pig brains out of the fridge and spray-painted the baby doll," Trent laughs. "Yeah, that was an interesting house!"

The pair stop in Canal Street Tavern, a tiny bar with a stage that owner Mick Montgomery grew into a staple of Dayton music, not to mention a checkpoint for national acts passing through the Midwest. Alt-rock acts such as Pixies and the Smashing Pumpkins played here in the early nineties. Decades earlier, so did Arlo Guthrie. There are tall tales, none of them confirmed, that Hank Williams also graced the tiny stage.

Bodine starts joking about the Battle of the Bands–style show Brainiac won in Dayton around 1992, which scored the group some free studio time. After twelve initial rounds in the competition, event organizers asked Brainiac, then still building out its setlist, to play a forty-five-minute set. They had about twenty minutes of material. (Bodine says, during the Battle of the Bands, they played a long-lost piece then called "Juan's Song," as well as covers of "Nausea" by X and "Miracle Time" by the Stooges.)

"Everybody loved us there, and we kept showing up," Bodine laughs.

Then, back at Canal Street, their attention turns to the bar, a Dayton music-scene fixture now filled with pinball machines. And memories.

Montgomery sold the Canal Tavern in 2013. After his 2018 death, the venue was remodeled as a pinball arcade and deli. The city renamed the street outside the venue in Montgomery's honor.

Trent and Bodine carefully walk along the tavern's wooden floors and wander over, past the pinball machines, to the walls at the back of the bar. Nearly every inch of the walls has been covered, shellacked really, in stickers promoting local bands from decades past.

A paper sign nearby reads, "Please respect and keep the integrity of these walls intact. No new stickers or signatures. Thank you!"

Flier for show at Canal Street Tavern. Courtesy of Michelle Bodine.

There's no sticker anywhere on the wall for Brainiac or the Breeders, whom Trent and Bodine remember playing to a pretty awesome crowd on a 1993 double bill at the tavern.

Neither of the pair can remember if they ever tried to plaster a sticker there. But both musicians dutifully read each band's name, seeing if they could drum up some memories or context to keep the band alive.

Flamingo Nosebleed. Triggerfish. Johnny Smoke. Pretty Mighty Mighty.

They're all gone now—or so the pair is guessing. Montgomery's old office, where he'd pay local bands whatever cut of the door he could, is now a custodial closet. The tavern's dressing room for bands is now part of a kitchen.

Throughout 2023, the surviving members of Brainiac embraced the idea of this biography, some text to add to the historical record and track their musical arc. When I approached them with questions, they each warmly answered and shared their stories. John Schmersal had his own thoughts on the narrative.

Above all, he didn't want it to just repeat the same old, tired story about a band on the brink of making it big instead collapsing after a tragic car crash took the life of their young, charismatic front man.

"You know, weird band starts to rise, was going to sign to a major label and gets cut short by the death of the main guy, basically," Schmersal says. "Everybody in this band brought something great to the table.

"What's great about our band is that we were an independent band," he adds. "We were truly an original band, and that's what was interesting about us and that's why our music still matters to people. I think it's a little lazy to do the 'Timmy Taylor was Brainiac' routine. Any band is obviously the sum of its parts. And everyone contributes something. And to say, 'Brainiac was Taylor,' I think is reductive."

It's hard not to make the argument that Tim Taylor might have budded into some sort of musical madman, more iconic than underground.

"He couldn't really turn it off, which to me is a big signifier. He just kind of lived [his music]," Trent says. "He was always creating this mindlessness, always going. And his songwriting was constantly evolving. In the documentary, Scott McCloud said something about how each record was reinventing itself. And that's what Tim was always doing. It was amazing. It was very obvious from the start that he was a pretty special dude."

But Brainiac might matter more now than ever, given an age where the musical playing field is both increasingly democratized and also, somehow, carefully narrated, Schmersal says.

"The thing that bugs me the most about music now is that, when you hear songs on the radio and stuff, it sounds already like a fucking car commercial or whatever," Schmersal chuckles. "To me, it doesn't sound original, it doesn't sound exciting. It doesn't sound weird or novel. And that bums me out. So that's kind of what I want to be remembered by. I want to be remembered for being really cut from a different cloth and taking our own route and making music that was truly original and different. That's why it mattered, you know."

The years since 1997 have not healed all wounds for the Brainiac family.

Linda Taylor still intensely misses her son.

"I mean, I've come to terms with it, but it's just an ache that never goes away. There's not a day I don't think about him or miss him," she tells me. "I don't know if I try to push feelings aside sometimes or not think about it. I just handle it by thinking about all the good memories.

"He meant everything to me," she adds. "Both my kids do."

Linda remembers the morning the officers came to her Dayton home to tell her about the accident. She heard a knock at the front door. It was around 7:00 a.m.—a little bit early for someone like the utility meter reader to be stopping by. She got to the door, opened it, and started walking the meter reader into her home.

But the meter reader didn't come that day.

"I realized, 'Wait a minute, this guy is not following me,'" she says. "And when he started talking, everything just kind of went numb in my head. Everything exploded. For a while I was just on autopilot, just not believing it.

"It's the most horrible thing in the world," she adds. "I don't know any parent that wouldn't give up their life for their kid. If there was any way I could say 'Take me, not him,' you do it. But life doesn't work out that way."

Twenty years passed until Linda Taylor came out again for a Brainiac show. The first one she caught was the fundraiser performance for the documentary at the Bell House in Brooklyn back in late 2017.

She admits it was hard, at first, to watch.

"It brings back memories of seeing them perform," she says. "And they get it."

Since the Brooklyn show, Linda has been religiously attending the Brainiac reunion live performances, just as she did the band's live sets in the nineties. Schmersal and others like to joke that she's the first person to show up in her Brainiac gear. Long gone, though, are those "Fuck Y'All, We're from Dayton" T-shirts.

"Tim's music is living on," Linda says, simply. "And, all those guys, I love 'em to death."

For one of the first times since the nineties, Brainiac, these underground legends, are getting their due, taking their victory lap.

She loves taking it all in. The excitement percolating around new fans streaming her son's music, a technology she never envisioned in the midnineties. The spirited live shows with the eclectic, multigenerational crowds. The carefully made documentary that traced Tim Taylor's rise and tragic fall.

"It all brings back really good memories of watching them perform," Linda says. "What I really love is watching younger audiences in their early twenties. Some of them weren't even born yet [at Brainiac's peak]—they're picking up and loving this music.

"That's really gratifying to me, to know that it's still out there," she says. "People are still enjoying Brainiac."

CHAPTER NOTES

Prologue: "A disaster scenario I cannot have"
DeLuca, Leo. "Why Brainiac Mattered, According to the Breeders, the Wrens, and More." *Pitchfork*, May 25, 2017. https://pitchfork.com/thepitch/1528-why-brainiac-mattered-according-to-the-breeders-the-wrens-and-more/

1. "Like Devo on acid"
Amter, Charlie. "Brainiac, the Great Lost Band of the '90s, Get Documentary Treatment in 'Transmissions After Zero.'" *Variety*, April 10, 2019. https://variety.com/2019/music/news/brainiac-great-lost-band-of-90s-documentary-transmissions-after-zero-1203186270/

Braithwaite, Stuart. *Spaceships over Glasgow: Mogwai, Mayhem and Misspent Youth*. London: Orion Publishing Group, 2022.

Ludwig, Jamie. "Brainiac: Transmissions After Zero." *Chicago Reader*, June 20, 2019. https://chicagoreader.com/film/brainiac-transmissions-after-zero/

Musical interlude: "Superdupersonic"
"*Hissing Prigs Review* from ULTRA WWW Magazine."
https://3ra1n1ac.com/reviews/ultra-www-magazine-hissing-prigs-review/

4. "Ride yourself away, each and every day"
Egan, Brian. "*Smack Bunny Baby Review.*" AllMusic.
https://www.allmusic.com/album/smack-bunny-baby-mw0000105713

Greer, Jim. "10 Best Albums of the Year You Didn't Hear." *Spin*, January 1994.

Punk Parent Dan. "Interview." *If You Have Scene, What We Have Zine*, April 1994.
https://3ra1n1ac.com/interviews/if-you-have-scene-what-we-have-zine-interview/

"The Story of Grass Records: From Brainiac to Wind-up and Creed." *Trout Fishing in Music*.
https://www.tumblr.com/troutfishinginmusic/642129824336445440

Woodlief, Mark. "Brainiac." *Trouser Press*.
https://trouserpress.com/reviews/brainiac/

5. "They were just getting bigger and bigger"
"Interview with Tim."
https://3ra1n1ac.com/interviews/interview-with-tim/

7. "Don't melt me down till the crisis is over"

"Nothing ever changes." Connor Choice, September 27, 2004.
https://web.archive.org/web/20040927114422/http://hissing-prigs-in-static-couture.connor-choice.com/

Sylvester, Nick. "Top 100 Albums of the 1990s." *Pitchfork*, November 16, 2003.
https://pitchfork.com/features/lists-and-guides/5923-top-100-albums-of-the-1990s/?page=3

Terich, Jeff. "Brainiac's 'Hissing Prigs in Static Couture' Is Built on Abrasive, Oddball Energy." *Treble Zine*, April 27, 2021.
https://www.treblezine.com/brainiac-hissing-prigs-static-couture-hall-of-fame/

8. "Electronic. And so aggressive."

DeLuca, Leo. "26 Years After Its Singer's Sudden Death, Brainiac (Briefly) Returns." *New York Times*, January 17, 2023.
https://www.nytimes.com/2023/01/17/arts/music/brainiac-predator-nominate.html

"'Hissing Prigs' Review from *CMJ* Magazine."
www.3ra1n1ac.com

9. "I want this to mean something"

Pirnia, Garin. *Rebels and Underdogs: The Story of Ohio Rock and Roll*. Bloomington: Indiana University Press, 2018.

Shiverdecker, Matt. "Well-versed: 5 Music Docs at SXSW

That Sang to Our Hearts." *Austin American-Statesman*, March 19, 2019. https://www.statesman.com/story/entertainment/music/sxsw/2019/03/19/well-versed-5-music-docs-at-sxsw-that-sang-to-our-hearts/5675330007/

Thrasher, Don. "'Heartbreak and Joy': Surviving Members of Dayton Band, Brainiac, Honor Late Leader." *Dayton Daily News*, February 24, 2023.

Milton Keynes UK
Ingram Content Group UK Ltd.
UKHW020815070524
442340UK00005B/228